123 Activities That Create Powerful Teachable Moments

ROPE

GAMES

Using a Finite Collection of Ropes to Facilitate

an Infinite Variety of Group Experiences

JIM CAIN

The Easy as 1-2-3 Series from Teamwork & Teamplay

jimcain@teamworkandteamplay.com

First Printing September 2013

Rope Games by Jim Cain
www.teamworkandteamplay.com

ISBN 978-0-9882046-1-4

A Teamwork & Teamplay Easy as 1-2-3 Publication

Table of Contents

An Introduction to Ropework & Ropeplay
Using Ropes to Create Teachable Moments
1. Openers, Icebreakers, Warm-Up Activities & Energizers
2. Team Challenges & Trust Building Activities
3. Tricks, Stunts, Puzzles & Other Challenges
4. Games Just for Fun
5. Reviewing Techniques & Closing Activities
6. Bonus Activities and More Rope Game Ideas
7. The Top Ten List & How to Make Your Own Rope Games Equipment
8. References and Resources
   Reference Books – A Bibliography
   Other Books by Jim Cain
   The Rope Games Kit
   About Jim Cain and Teamwork & Teamplay
   About the Easy as 1-2-3 Series of Books
   The Value of a Little Red Rope
   For More Information

"One of the simplest and most enduring tools ever devised is rope. For centuries we have used ropes to sail our ships of exploration, to carry our burdens, to lash together our dreams, and to facilitate our play. It is fitting indeed that we should take ropes with us, as a valued tool for creating our future."

Jim Cain
Rope Games

An Introduction to Ropework & Ropeplay

There have been several significant events that inspired the development of the rope games shared in this book. The first event happened more than two decades ago when Patrick English Farrell presented a workshop at the mid-Atlantic AEE conference in Richmond, Virginia entitled "Ninety Minutes and a Rope." I was inspired by the utility that could be found in a single piece of rope. Who knew that a single conference workshop would become such an inspiration more than twenty years after it was presented? That is the power of a great idea!

Just a few years later, I found myself at a conference hosted by Bradford Woods in Indiana. Dr. Tom Smith was presenting a morning workshop that utilized only a single piece of equipment – a fifteen foot long segment of tubular climbing webbing which he called a 'raccoon circle.' For four hours the twenty participants in Tom's workshop played dozens of valuable games using only this single simple tool. As a result, Tom and I collaborated on the first commercially published Book on Raccoon Circles, the Revised and Expanded Edition and several international projects since (including translations for Japan, China, Greece and Spain). In addition, an internet collection of Raccoon Circle activities was created and has been downloaded over two million times in more than one hundred different countries around the world. Raccoon Circles have truly become the 'world wide webbing!'

The third inspirational event occurred more recently when one of my airline flights was delayed due to inclimate weather. After hours of delay, I finally arrived at my destination at 2am, but without any of my luggage. On the way to my hotel, I stopped at a 24-hour department store and purchased two packs of index cards, some colorful markers, a can of tennis balls and two 100 foot long lengths of rope. Six hours later, I successfully facilitated my first teambuilding program for a new client, using only these simple props. Several of the activities I brainstormed that evening can be found in this book.

Since these early inspirational moments in my career as a teacher, trainer, facilitator, camp professional and author, I have created and collected dozens of activities that use ropes and cordage of all kinds to create significant teachable moments. I called my first published collection of these activities The Ropework & Ropeplay Kit – which was an accurate description of the contents - ten different varieties of rope, string, shock cord, webbing and other cordage that could be used to facilitate over 300 activities. I liked the use of the words work and play in the title, and their similarity to my corporate moniker Teamwork & Teamplay.

Most recently, two new inspirations have returned and focused my attention on this book project. The first of these was my decision to take a one-year sabbatical during which I created, collected, researched and fabricated more than a dozen new rope activities. Having something new to share, especially something simple that creates the opportunity for significant teachable moments, is truly a joy.

The second inspiration came during the creation of the first book in the Teamwork & Teamplay Easy as 1-2-3 series - a no prop activity book entitled 'Find Something To Do!' During the writing of that book I was reminded that it is the quality of the activities contained and not the quantity that determines the value of a book. With that in mind, I was encouraged to share what I believe are the 'best of the best' rope games and activities from the myriads in my collection.

So you now have before you a collection of my favorite, newest and best team and community building activities using rope from around the world. I hope these activities bring you many hours of joyful play, excellent facilitation, valuable training and many, many teachable moments.

Jim Cain
Rope Games

Using Ropes to Create Teachable Moments

In my work as a teacher, trainer, facilitator and group leader I employ a variety of techniques to achieve the program goals of my participants and clients. Most of these techniques involve teamwork, adventure-based learning, experiential education and active learning methodologies. One of the most profound ways to engage a group is to incorporate activities and group exercises that create powerful teachable moments.

A teachable moment is an opportunity for a group to learn from a particularly insightful or significant event that has occurred during a group experience. Such an event could be a breakthrough moment when a group discovers a technique which leads to the successful completion of a task. But success is not a prerequisite. Teachable moments can occur in the middle of a task or during a moment of failure.

The idea of using a variety of ropes to create teachable moments is not new. Apprenticeships for sailors and seamen of all kinds often involved learning the ropes. A century ago, this phrase referred to a new recruit on a sailing vessel learning how to climb and handle the many ropes that operated the ship's sails. For the purpose of this book, learning the ropes refers to understanding how to facilitate powerful group activities that explore a wide variety of topics while using a unique collection of rope, string and other forms of cordage.

Many other professions also incorporate rope and teachable moments in their trade. Knot tying has long been an essential skill for tradesmen of all kinds. Mountain climbers know the ropes, as do fishermen, sailors, weavers and many more trades that utilize thread, string and rope in the completion of their work. Children around the world have played string games and jumped rope. Even physicists and mathematicians have joined the ranks of those who use ropes to create teachable moments with their theoretical frameworks of string theory and knot theory. If all these professions can find utility in ropes, surely there is room for educators and group leaders of all kinds to do the same.

One of the most significant reasons I employ rope games in my trainings is to create a sensory rich learning environment. Allowing participants to physically touch a rope as part of an activity provides more sensory input than speech or vision alone. Tactile learners and haptic learners (those who learn through touch and are also stimulated by movement and sensory input) specifically benefit from this style of learning. Some of the most skilled haptic practitioners are magicians who incorporate rope tricks into many of their presentations. Magicians often create 'ah-hah!' moments with ropes in their tricks. I try to do the same.

It is possible to play many of the rope activities in this book as pure games and nothing more. Play all by itself is also a worthy endeavor. But these activities have the potential to be more than just a pastime and much more than just a game. They can be used to explore valuable life skills and to develop career skills as varied as consensus building, communication, decision-making, resource management, trust building, creative problem solving and teamwork. How can these rope games do all that? By providing the opportunity for participants to encounter teachable moments along the way.

To close, I will borrow the wisdom of a dear friend of mine, Dr. Tom Smith (co-author of *The Book of Raccoon Circles*). When Tom invites audiences to join together around a Raccoon Circle, he simply says, 'connect up!' Being physically connected to others within a group builds community in a way that goes beyond words alone. The give and take required to move an object when a dozen people are all pulling in different directions quickly becomes evident (see the Bull Ring activity in this book). I think rope is not just a practical tool for creating teachable moments, it is an ideal tool! Try a few of the activities in this book for yourself, and I believe you will quickly find out just how powerful it can be to use ropes to create your own teachable moments.

Chapter One
Openers, Icebreakers, Warm-Ups & Energizers

This chapter contains activities that are perfect for the beginning stages of an event. Icebreakers for the opening session of a conference, warm-up activities to get your group moving, and communication starters and energizers to invigorate and motivate your participants. Keep each of your icebreaking activities to less than seven minutes long and you'll improve the energy and engagement of your audience!

Group Sizes

At the start of each chapter in this book you'll find a list of the activities contained there, the category, theme or teachable moment of each activity and the ideal group size (which is generally one of the following):

Individuals (1 person)   Small Groups (5-8)
Partners (2 people)   Medium Groups (9-25)
Triads (3 people)   Large Groups (>25)
Foursome (4 people)   XL Groups (>100)

Openers, Icebreakers, Warm-Ups & Energizers

No.	Name	Category	Group Size
1-1	What is a Raccoon Circle?	Information	Any
1-2	Wrapped Around My Finger & The Inchworm	Icebreaker	Small
1-3	Where Ya From Where Ya Been?	Icebreaker	Small
1-4	Twice Around the Block	Icebreaker	Small
1-5	My Lifeline	Icebreaker	Small
1-6	All My Life's a Circle	Icebreaker	Small
1-7	Believe It or Knot	Icebreaker	Small/Med
1-8	The Story of Your Name	Icebreaker	Any
1-9	Over Here!	Icebreaker	Med/Large

Individuals (1 person)   Small Groups (5-8)
Partners (2 people)   Medium Groups (9-25)
Triads (3 people)   Large Groups (>25)
Foursome (4 people)   XL Groups (>100)

No.	Name	Category	Group Size
1-10	Goal Lines & Spokes	Goal Setting	Small/Med
1-11	Four Corners	Icebreaker	Med/Large
1-12	The Bus & Which Side of the Road?	Icebreaker	Med/Large
1-13	Asking Questions	Icebreaker	Any
1-14	Team Yoga	Warm-Up	Small/Med
1-15	100 Ways to Cross a Circle	Icebreaker Energizer	Med/Large
1-16	The Fifty Yard Scream	Energizer	Med/Large
1-17	Grand Prix Racing	Energizer	Multiple Small Groups
1-18	My Story	Icebreaker	Small

For additional openers, icebreakers, warm-up activities and energizers, including many that require no equipment at all, see the book *Find Something To Do!* by Jim Cain. ISBN 978-0-9882046-0-7. This book contains over 130 activities that require zero props!

1-1 What is a Raccoon Circle?

One of the most versatile ropes in the Rope Games collection is a 15 foot (4.6 meter) long piece of tubular climbing webbing known as a Raccoon Circle. With this single piece of webbing you can facilitate hundreds of small group activities, including icebreakers and opening activities in this first chapter and many additional activities throughout this book. There are two common ways to use a Raccoon Circle: knotted (so that the webbing is tied to make a circle) or unknotted (forming a long line instead of a circle). To make a circle from the Raccoon Circle webbing, you will need to tie a water knot.

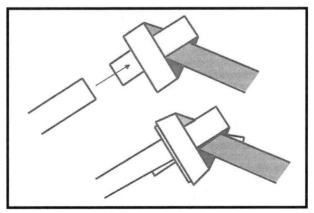

A water knot is ideal for webbing and is made by first tying a loose overhand knot with one end of the webbing and then passing the other end of the webbing backwards through this overhand knot.

You can create even larger circles by using water knots to join several Raccoon Circles together.

You can find a free PDF document of Raccoon Circle activities, program ideas and suggestions at the Teamwork & Teamplay website:

www.teamworkandteamplay.com

For more Raccoon Circle information, Kendall/Hunt publishes *The Revised and Expanded Book of Raccoon Circles* by Jim Cain and Tom Smith. For more information visit:
www.kendallhunt.com (1-800-228-0810)

1-2 Wrapped Around My Finger

Wrapped Around My Finger is my favorite painless icebreaker. This activity is simple to facilitate and is a very engaging opening activity.

Begin with one unknotted Raccoon Circle for each group of six people. One person in the group begins wrapping the webbing around their index finger and while doing so tells the group some information about themselves (where they were born, family members, school experiences, childhood pets, dreams, goals, favorite foods, etc.) The goal is for this person to continue talking until the webbing is completely wrapped around their finger. When they reach the end, they allow the webbing to unwind and pass it along to the next person in the group.

This particular activity provides plenty of time for folks to share information about themselves in a relaxed small group setting. It combines a kinesthetic activity with a language activity for exploring multiple intelligence opportunities and whole brain learning possibilities. There is a popular theory that for folks that may be a bit shy about speaking in public, the action of wrapping the webbing around their finger occupies that portion of the brain where nervousness occurs. By wrapping and talking at the same time, the speech control center becomes less inhibited and the person talking is typically more relaxed.

The length of a Raccoon Circle allows more than a minute of communication, which means you'll learn quite a bit more about a person than just their name and where they live.

The Inchworm

If you enjoy Wrapped Around My Finger, but the time goes by too quickly for your participants to share their story, The Inchworm technique will allow a bit more time for each person.

Instead of wrapping a Raccoon Circle around your finger while talking, participants pinch the Raccoon Circle between their first finger and thumb of one hand and then the other, over and over again as they 'inch' along the length of the Raccoon Circle. This technique will allow a bit more time for each person to introduce themselves.

1-3 Where Ya From?
Where Ya Been?

During one memorable icebreaker session, a participant mentioned that they were born in Scotland. Another member of the group wasn't familiar with the geography of that region and so the outline of Scotland was created using a knotted Raccoon Circle. Then several participants told stories about their travels to Scotland, which led to the creation of the following activity.

Where Ya From? Where Ya Been? has become a great way for each person in the group to share 'their story.' One at a time, they create the outline of where they are from, or similarly someplace they have recently visited, and then tell stories about these places.

21

Several key elements make this activity a 'painless' icebreaker. First, while one person is describing their geographical location, the other members of the group are generally looking at the map rather than at the person talking. Next, other group members that have visited the same location can add their stories. And finally, the geography presented by each person is generally quite familiar to them, which allows their presentation to be personal and familiar.

Group members are encouraged to stay connected with the Raccoon Circle as they create the map used for each person's story. If the map is created on the ground instead of in the air, active participants become mere spectators. For higher levels of engagement, keep group members in contact with the Raccoon Circle.

1-4 Twice Around the Block

Here is a playful icebreaker that allows the members of each small group to decide how long a person talks while introducing themselves.

To begin, you'll need a knotted Raccoon Circle for each group. While the rest of the group holds on, the person nearest the knot lets go. As this person introduces themself, the rest of the team listens attentively as they slowly pass the knot to the right around the circle. When the knot reaches the person talking the first time (once around the block) their time is half gone. When the knot reaches the person talking the second time, their turn is over.

In this activity, group members control the time for each person by controlling the speed of the knot moving around the circle. If they are enjoying the story, they can slow down the movement of the knot. They can also speed up the knot to bring the introduction to a close more quickly.

Groups often laugh as they speed up the movement of the knot, but then typically allow the person talking to respectfully finish their introduction. Fun for everyone and especially empowering for each group to feel in control of the length of time each member of their group talks.

1-5 My Life Line

This activity begins by creating a straight line on the ground with an unknotted Raccoon Circle. Consider this line a 'timeline' of your life. The members of each small group walk together along the line as one person shares some of the major milestones of their life. When they reach the present day, there will still be some portion of the line left untraveled. Here they can share some of their future plans and goals. When one person completes their story, the group returns to the beginning of the rope and another member of the group shares the story of their lifeline. Some participants suggest adding a few curves to the lifeline, for those moments in life that did not go according to plan.

1-6 All My Life's a Circle

Here is a fun way to add movement to an icebreaking activity. Consider this as a circular version of My Life Line from the previous page.

In small groups of five to eight people, one person begins to tell the story of their life as they walk around the outside perimeter of a knotted Raccoon Circle on the ground. The members of the group follow along as the storyteller continues sharing some of the major events of their life.

Once the first person has completed a lap (or perhaps several) the next person begins, walking in the opposite direction (so as not to make the group dizzy). Continue this activity until all members of the group have had the opportunity to share.

1-7 Believe It or Knot

Begin this icebreaker with the entire group holding a knotted Raccoon Circle. Pass the knot to the right around the group. When someone at random says "stop," the person nearest the knot is invited to disclose some interesting fact about themselves, such as: "I have a twin sister!" It is now the responsibility of the rest of the group members to discuss and decide whether they believe this information to be true or false. Group members can ask the person speaking a total of three questions. After discussion, the group gives their opinion of the validity or falseness of the disclosure and then the person providing the comment tells whether their statement was true or false. After this, the speaker says "left" or "right" and the knot once again begins moving around the circle. When someone says 'stop,' the next person nearest the knot is invited to disclose something to the group.

This is the type of activity that can be repeated even with the same group, because there is an endless supply of disclosures that can be made, especially as trust builds within a group.

Thanks to Mike Anderson for sharing this
rope variation of Two Truths and a Lie.

1-8 The Story of Your Name

Whenever I am in a culturally diverse audience, I like to share this activity. Begin by inviting your group to sit comfortably around a rope circle.

Everyone has a story related to their name. Some of us are named after a favorite relative, a close family friend or perhaps even someone famous. Our middle names are significant too. For this activity, invite everyone to share the story of their full name. How they came to have it. If they like it or not. Encourage participants to end with the phrase "please call me…. *their name of choice here*," and invite the group to practice calling them by the name they choose.

In this way, each person will have the opportunity to say how they like to be addressed, and what is positive, interesting or even unusual about their name.

The Story of Your Name is a deceptively simple opening activity that can have a significant effect on the day-to-day operations of an organization and the members of a group. This activity creates a safe place where participants can tell the story of how they came to have their name. The underlying and sometimes overlooked potential of this activity is the opportunity to create a theme of respect and significance to the name by which people would like to be addressed. In other words, The Story of Your Name is not only a convenient way for people to remember each other's names, but also to build a community of respect for each other in the process.

1-9 Over Here!

Here is an activity that will create an atmosphere of inclusion and rapidly mix your entire audience. Begin by placing several knotted Raccoon Circles on the ground and invite participants to stand within one of these circles. Next identify one specific characteristic for the members of each group, such as the tallest person and have this person step out of the circle. When this person steps away from the group they have become a 'free agent' and other groups can call out, *'over here, over here!'* to attract them to join their circle.

Here are a few basic rules. You can attract the same person back to your circle. You can invite more than one person to join you. You can go out and recruit if you like, but your recruiting efforts must be non-contact (i.e. you cannot pull another person into your group).

Additional group characteristics include: length of hair, most articles of jewelry, largest or smallest shoe size, wearing the most green, number of brothers and sisters, coolest watch, cleanest shoes...

Thanks to Chris Cavert for sharing this wonderful activity, which he calls See Ya!

1-10 Personal Goal Lines

Place a single short rope in front of each participant with three strategically placed knots along the length. The first knot at the near end represents the beginning of the program. A second knot midway along the rope represents the middle of the program. The final knot at the far end of the rope represents the conclusion of the program. Using this simple visual model as a tool, each person can now discuss their personal goals for the program. Where do they want to be at the end of the experience? Where do they want to be by the mid-point (lunchtime)? Where are they now, at the beginning of the day? What events need to happen to achieve their personal goals for the day?

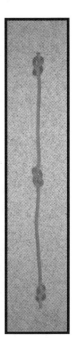

At the completion of the event, participants can be invited to assess how close they were to achieving their personal goals for this program.

Spokes

If you would like the members of your group to set personal goals and understand the impact these have on the entire group, position the ropes like the spokes of a wheel, so they all meet at the center. Then ask each member of the group to consider how their personal goals match up with the goals of the entire group. Are their personal goals and the goals of the group in concert or conflict with each other? Will achieving their personal goals help or hinder the achievement of the goals of the entire group? Is there anything they can do to reconcile their personal goals and the goals of the group so that both can be achieved?

You can leave these rope spokes in place for the day and occasionally revisit them as a group. Participants may wish to modify their original goals as a result of some of the teachable moments they have experienced.

Thanks to Roger Greenaway for sharing these goal-setting activities. You can find these and other creative ideas at: www.reviewing.co.uk

1-11 Four Corners

The concept for this opening activity is simple enough - with a long rope or multiple unknotted Raccoon Circles, divide the available space into four quadrants. Next inform your audience what each quadrant represents and ask everyone to stand within the quadrant of their preference.

For example, if the quadrants represent four styles of leadership, you might identify the quadrants as: orchestra conductor, military drill sergeant, baseball coach or mountain guide. Once everyone has chosen their appropriate quadrant, invite them to have a conversation with other quadrant members about this topic including the questions provided on the following page.

If the classification of music is chosen, the four quadrants might represent: rock, rap, country and classical. After participants join a group, ask the group to discuss why they chose this particular style of music. The facilitator can also ask the group to perform a piece of music from their category of choice.

Additional themes for the four quadrants can be found on the next page.

Themes for Four Corners

Sports (Basketball, Soccer, Football, Baseball)
Create a cheer for your sport.

Vacations (Beach, Mountain, Big City, Cruise)
What do you plan to bring along with you?

Food (Hamburgers, Fried Chicken, Tunafish, Veggie Burger) or something a bit more unusual, such as (Cous Cous, Sushi, Broccoli, Mountain Oysters) What goes along with each food?

Vehicles (pickup, sports car, mini van, SUV)
Discuss features & optional equipment.

Travel (North, East, South, West)
What would you bring with you?

News (Newspaper, Radio, Television, Internet)
Discuss recent events and issues.

Movies (Action, Adventure, Romance, Classics)
Act out a scene from your favorite movie.

Websites (news, TV shows, games, social networking) What is your favorite website?

1-12 The Bus

Begin this activity by placing two unknotted Raccoon Circles parallel (to form the side outline of your 'bus'). Next, invite participants to step onboard. As you drive down the road seeing various things along the way, invite your passengers to disembark on either side of the bus, according to their preference. First stop, ice cream. On one side Chocolate, on the other side Vanilla. Now choose and step off the bus.

As with many of these conversational activities, once you have grouped folks together by a theme, invite them to discuss some component of this theme, such as their favorite place to eat ice cream, or toppings they would add.

Then invite them to get back on the bus, and travel again (perhaps over a bumpy road this time) to your next destination and the next choice: Pets this time..... cats or dogs?

As you continue on your journey, consider other choices such as: save money vs. spend money, bus driver vs. bus rider, sky diving vs. deep sea diving, problem solver vs. problem maker, etc.

In addition to being just a bus driver, you might also be a tour guide, providing some interesting facts and reacting to imaginery things you bump into along the way.

Which Side of the Road Are You On?

Would you rather......donate money to a worthy cause or donate your time to help them in person?

If you would like to incorporate a higher level of decision making (compared to the previous activity - The Bus), consider sharing questions that require a bit more thinking or that contain an ethical dilemma. 'Would you rather?' questions are especially suited to this activity. Are you more like: summer or winter, early morning or late night, cash or credit, a stroll on the beach or a stroll in the rain, sunrise or sunset, movie theatre or DVD at home, paperclip or rubberband, paper book or electronic book, pencil or pen, library or bookstore, work or play....?

For even more questions to ponder and interesting choices to make, read: *The Book of Questions* by Gregory Stock, *If Anybody Asks Me...* by Larry Eckert, *Are you More Like? 1001 Colorful Quandaries for Quality Conversations* by Chris Cavert, *If - Questions for the Game of Life* by McFarland and Saywell, *The Conversation Pie* and *Think Twice - A Collection of Choices* by Nicholaus and Lowrie, *Would You Rather...?* by Heimberg and Gomberg, *You Gotta Be Kidding?* by Horn, Ring and Fierz, *Zobmondo - The Outrageous Book of Bizarre Choices* by Randy Horn, and *Question of the Day* by Al Katkowshy (there is also an smartphone app of this same name!)

1-13 Asking Questions

One of the simplest ways to encourage participation in large groups is to break the group into smaller and infinitely more manageable pieces. Discussion groups of four or five people are ideal and a group of this size can easily fit or sit within the perimeter of a Raccoon Circle. Here are some of my favorite questions for small group discussions.

1. If you could have one million of anything, except money, what would you choose?
2. What is the most interesting thing you have ever found?
3. Of all the animals you have known in your life, which one was your favorite?
4. What movie have you seen more than once?
5. What is the most valuable thing you have ever learned?
6. Who was your favorite teacher and why?
7. What would you do if you knew you could not fail?
8. What can you do in your dreams that you cannot do in real life?
9. If you received a new MP3 music player, what is the first song you would download?

10. What is the best advice you were ever given?
11. If you could go back in time, what would you change?
12. What has really surprised you lately?
13. Have you collected anything in your lifetime?
14. What is the last thing you recommended?
15. What storms have you weathered?
16. What can you do better than anyone else?
17. Who inspires you?
18. What is the oldest thing you own?
19. What have you mastered recently?
20. What was the best meal of your life so far?
21. Who is your most unique relative and why?
22. What challenges you?
23. What have you downloaded lately?
24. When you were a child, what did you want to be when you grew up?
25. Name one thing everyone should do in their life.
26. How many different countries have you visited and which one was your favorite?
27. Sum up your entire life in just five words.
28. Which is your favorite pair of shoes and why?
29. Tell me about your first job.
30. Describe a perfect day.
31. What is the best thing that has ever happened to you?
32. What is your favorite daydream?

1-14 Team Yoga

While a majority of the activities in this first chapter are conversational, this next one is purely physical and makes a great warm up activity. Provide each small group a knotted Raccoon Circle and invite them to invent their own artistic yoga positions, movements and stretches while connected together with the Raccoon Circle.

A special thanks to Tom Andrews for sharing his bunched lycra tube version of this activity.

39

1-15 100 Ways to Cross a Circle

This activity comes from the field of theatre sports and is excellent for mixing the members of a group and encouraging a bit of theatrical creativity in the process. Begin by creating a large circular open space with a long rope. Next, invite every participant to cross through the center of the circle to the other side moving in a different manner. If the first person imitates a waiter carrying a tray, the person they approach on the opposite side of the circle must cross the circle in a different manner, such as rowing a canoe. The more visual and funny the presentation, the more excitment and energy created within the group.

A second variation of this activity is to invite several volunteers to each invent a unique method for crossing the circle and to 'pass off" this same method to another person on the far side of the circle. So a juggler passes off the three juggling balls to the person they approach on the far side of the circle, who then crosses the circle as a juggler and passes off these three juggling balls to the person they approach on the opposite side of the circle, and on, and on... Just watch out for the other creative folks also passing through the center of the circle.

1-16 The Fifty Yard Scream

This is one of the quickest ways to increase the energy level in any group, provided you have lots of outdoor space and don't mind some significant noise! Place a long rope on the ground as a starting line and ask everyone to stand behind it.

Next, invite everyone to take a deep breath and then run forwards as far as they can while screaming at the top of their lungs. When they need to take a breath, they stop running as well. Give them a few minutes to rest and then ask them to scream and return (and see if they can make it all the way back to their original starting position with one breath).

This activity is both an aerobic challenge and an excellent energizer. Depending on the fitness level of your group, some participants may travel substantially further than others.

41

1-17 Grand Prix Racing

Here is one of the best activities I know for building energy and enthusiasm within a group. You'll need a knotted Raccoon Circle for each group of 5-8 participants. The more groups you have, the greater the energy generated.

The 'race car' for this activity is the water knot on each Raccoon Circle. Team members use their hands to move the knot quickly to the right or left around the circle. This activity can be performed while participants are seated or standing. The start and finish line for each race is the person nearest the knot.

To begin, share the following information with your audience:

Ladies and Gentlemen! It is summertime, and that can mean only one thing - Grand Prix Racing! Now I know that you are all race fans and just the thought of a race makes your heart beat faster, so listen carefully to these rules. First, when I say that we're going to have a race, your response is a loud, "Yahoo!" Next I'll say, start your engines! and I want to hear your best race car sounds (audience practices making race car revving engine, shifting gears and braking sounds). Finally, with so many cars on the track today, it will be difficult to see which group finishes their race first, so we'll need a sign indicating when your group is finished. That sign is to raise your hands (and the Raccoon Circle) above your heads and yell "Yesssssssssss!"

Now let's all take one slow practice lap to make sure we all know the rules. We're going to have a race! (Crowd replies, "yahoo!"). Start your engines! (Crowd makes race car sounds). One practice lap to the right. Ready? Steady? Go! (Each race team slowly moves their knot counterclockwise around the circle, and yells, "Yes!" when they finish this lap).

The Raccoon Circle Grand Prix Championship has a total of four races (five if you count the practice lap and even more possibilities if you are really creative).

The first race is a single lap race to the right, with the knot traveling once around the circle to the right (counterclockwise). The second race is a two lap race to the left (clockwise) around the circle. The third race consists of one lap to the right and then a quick reverse with another lap back to the left. The final race of the series is a "winner take all" championship race, with two laps to the right (counterclockwise), a quick pitstop (where everyone drops the Raccoon

44

Circle to the floor, individuals rotate 360 degrees (spin) and then pick up the Raccoon Circle again) and completes the course with one lap to the left (clockwise).

One interesting Grand Prix variation is to create a figure eight racetrack instead of the typical oval shape. This geometry requires some participants to shift the webbing in different directions from their neighbors, depending on where they are placed along the raceway. This is a great opportunity to discuss having a common vision and knowing which direction the team is moving.

1-18 My Story

A wonderful technique for storytelling is to provide a collection of props (such as the various cordage in the Rope Games kit) and then ask a storyteller to create a visual interpretation of their story using these props.

First, provide the storyteller with all the cordage from the Rope Games kit. Allow them a few minutes to create a visual interpretation of what they would like to convey. Then ask them to share their story and identify what the various elements of their rope model signify. Audience members are free to ask questions, suggest modifications and explore each element created by the storyteller.

For a terrific variation of this storytelling activity, see the activity Story Ropes in Chapter Six (www.margemalwitz.blogspot.com).

MRT (moral recognation therapy) and some forms of family and relationship therapy use pictures and objects as tools for storytelling. Metalog (an experiential tool company in Germany) has created an excellent storytelling and coaching tool, known as the Solution Board. For more information visit: www.metalog.co.uk.

Chapter Two
Team Challenges &
Trust Building Activities

This chapter contains activities for challenging groups and building trust. From simple and cerebral problem solving situations to complex and physically challenging initiatives, you'll find a wide variety of opportunities here for working and playing together as a group.

Some Thoughts About Safety

While most of the activities in this section involve slow movements and careful interactions between participants, the very nature of adventure-based teambuilding and trust building activities involves some element of risk, and as such suggests the need for appropriate spotting and appropriate settings, such as level, obstacle-free programming space and suitably selected partners and teams. If you are unfamiliar or uncertain about the appropriate safety guidelines for any of these activities, do not attempt them!

Team Challenges & Trust Building Activities

No.	Name	Category	Group Size
2-1	Bull Ring & Candelabra	Teamwork	Medium or Large
2-2	Bull Ring 3-D	Teamwork	Medium
2-3	Going Fishin'	Teamwork	Small
2-4	Write On	Teamwork	Small
2-5	Snap!	Teamwork	Small
2-6	Blind Square	Teamwork	Medium
2-7	Unblind Square	Leadership Teamwork	Medium or Large
2-8	Tree of Knots	Teamwork	Small
2-9	2B or Knot 2B	Consensus	Medium
2-10	Disconnected	Consensus	Medium
2-11	Not Knots	Consensus	Medium
2-12	Missing Link	Consensus	Medium
2-13	Stretching the Limit	Prob. Solv. Teamwork	Small
2-14	Handcuffs & Shackles	Prob. Solv. Teamwork	Partners
2-15	Pot of Gold & Toxic Waste	Prob. Solv. Teamwork	Medium

No.	Name	Category	Group Size
2-16	Interference	Communication	Large
2-17	All Aboard & High Tide	Prob. Solv.	Small or Medium
2-18	Photo Finish	Prob. Solv.	Small
2-19	Moving To Extinction	Prob. Solv.	Medium or Large
2-20	Traffic Circle	Prob. Solv.	Medium
2-21	Keys to Communication	Prob. Solv.	Small or Medium
2-22	Traffic Jam & People Movers	Prob. Solv.	Small
2-23	Longest Line	Teamwork	Small
2-24	10 x 10 x 10	Teamwork	Medium
2-25	Spider Web Variations	Teamwork Prob. Solv.	Small or Medium
2-26	Over the Fence	Teamwork Prob. Solv.	Small
2-27	Worm Hole	Teamwork	Medium
2-28	Window of Opportunity	Teamwork Prob. Solv.	Small
2-29	Electric Box	Teamwork	Small
2-30	Circle the Circle	Teamwork	Medium

No.	Name	Category	Group Size
2-31	Inside / Out	Prob. Solv.	Small
2-32	On Target	Teamwork	Small
2-33	Blind Find	Teamwork	Trios
2-34	Cross the Line	Conflict	Partners
2-35	Rock Around the Clock	Teamwork Prob. Solv.	Small
2-36	Alphabet Soup	Teamwork	Small
2-37	Match Cards	Character	Small
2-38	Minefield & Lighthouse	Communication	Partners
2-39	Reaching for Your Goals	Goal Setting	Small
2-40	Shape Up	Teamwork	Small
2-41	A Knot Between Us	Teamwork	Small
2-42	Knot Our Problem	Teamwork Prob. Solv.	Small
2-43	Tossing Pizza	Teamwork	Small

Individuals (1 person)	Small Groups (5-8)
Partners (2 people)	Medium Groups (9-25)
Triads (3 people)	Large Groups (>25)
Foursome (4 people)	XL Groups (>100)

No.	Name	Category	Group Size
2-44	Chain Gang	Teamwork	Small
2-45	Jumping Rope	Teamwork	Small
2-46	The Clock	Teamwork	Small
2-47	Line Up	Teamwork	Small
2-48	Spiral Labyrinth	Commun- ication	Partners
2-49	A Work of Art	Communic.	Small
2-50	Yurt Circle	Teamwork	Small
2-51	Jump the River	Teamwork	Small
2-52	Shoelaces	Teamwork	Partners
2-53	Tightrope	Spotting	Sm.-Med.
2-54	Trust Lift	Trust	Small
2-55	Trust Walk	Trust	Small
2-56	The Maze	Teamwork	Small
2-57	London Bridge	Teamwork	Sm.-Med.
2-58	Twins	Teamwork	Small
2-59	Need Help?	Prob. Solv.	Small
2-60	Exit Strategy	Prob. Solv.	Small
2-61	Linearity	Teamwork	Small
2-62	Outside The Box	Teamwork Creativity	Small
2-63	Bull Ring Variations	Teamwork Creativity	Small

2-1 Bull Ring

The Bull Ring is presented first in this chapter because it is one of the simplest and most valuable teambuilding props ever invented. With 8-12 pieces of colorful string and a metal ring, you have the ideal tennis ball transport device.

The goal of this activity is to transport a ball while encountering some challenges along the way (such as passing through a doorway or navigating under a picnic table).

If you have multiple Bull Ring teams, invite them to make all the balls touch in mid-air, while everyone is holding onto the end of a string. Or allow them to transport a variety of objects, such as a golf ball, ping pong ball, billiard ball, croquet ball or large ice cube.

Construct a candelabra made from PVC tubing and connectors and you have the ideal tool to bring several Bull Ring teams together for a grand finale.

2-2 Bull Ring 3-D

A 3-D Bull Ring is made with strings and a tube instead of a metal ring. If you have limited space to move around this variation of Bull Ring is ideal. Transporting a tennis ball even a short distance with this device requires a significantly higher level of skill and perseverance than the standard Bull Ring. You might want to give your team a chance to practice BEFORE placing a tennis ball on top of this 3-D Bull Ring.

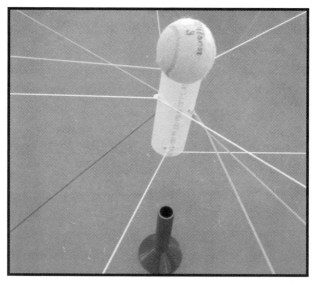

2-3 Goin' Fishin'

I created this variation of Bull Ring as part of a character education program. I replaced the metal ring with a wooden block and attached several hardware hooks to it. Next I found several wooden fish at my local craft store and attached a metal eyescrew to each. Then I invited my team to go fishing. On the back of each fish was a character word which the team discovered when they caught the fish. One fish was designed to fall off every time it was hooked. The word on the back - Perseverance! For a higher level of complexity, challenge your team to pick up a set mouse trap, without setting it off. A significant challenge that most groups can accomplish.

2-4 Write On!

Here is another Bull Ring with a twist. This time the metal ring is replaced with a section of a foam noodle that holds a colorful marker. Groups can write a message by working together, or transverse a maze (without crossing any lines) or drive a grand prix raceway without drawing outside the race course lines. A PVC tube version of Write On is also shown here. This model has a bit more control than the string and foam noodle version.

2-5 SNAP!

The band for this activity is made from 40 inches (1 meter) of 3/4 inch (19mm) wide elastic tied into a circle with a water knot. The challenge is for a circle of 5-10 people to stretch the band outward and then let go simultaneously so that the band snaps into the very center of the circle. If the timing is off by even a split second, the band typically ends up outside the circle or headed for the team member that was last to let go.

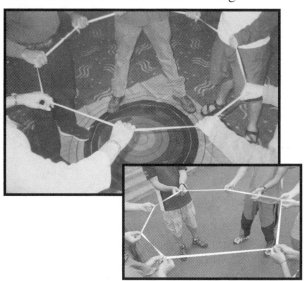

2-6 Blind Square

Begin this classic teambuilding activity by asking for one member of the group to observe (but not assist) the group and then blindfold the remaining participants. Next, place a long rope nearby. Instruct the group to find the rope and create a perfect square with it. Be sure to conduct this activity in a large, open space, free of any obstacles.

My favorite scenario for this activity is to inform the group that they have wandered off the hiking trail and darkness has fallen. Creating a perfect square with a light-reflective rope will help the search party find them.

For a higher level of challenge, you can add a few randomly placed knots or loops in the rope (the group will wonder if these have any significance).

2-7 Unblind Square

No blindfolds are needed for this sighted but still challenging version of creating shapes with rope. Begin by inviting your participants to each grasp a long rope. Next, ask them to connect the ends of the rope together with a knot. Throughout this activity, group members are allowed to slide their hands along the length of the rope, but they cannot let go or move past any other person.

Show one person in the group an illustration of a perfect square. Instruct them to lead the group (without letting go) in creating this shape with the rope. Provide feedback on their leadership performance. Did they, for example, just give instructions (telling), or did they communicate the exact shape to the group (shared vision)?

Next, show another person the second illustration (a bowtie-like shape) and ask them to lead the group. Again, process their leadership capabilities. Then show the entire group the third illustration (the three triangle hazard symbol), and invite them to work together to create this more challenging shape. Conclude by showing the group the star image and ask them to create this shape with the rope. The star is a very challenging shape, especially with a rope that has already been tied into a circle. But who tied that knot? The facilitator, no! The participants themselves. And so they are free to untie it if they wish. Debrief this activity based upon the leadership, communication, problem solving and teamwork capabilities of the group.

2-8 Tree of Knots

You will need a long rope placed around a tree or pole for this teambuilding activity. Place half the group at each end of the rope. The task is for the group to tie a square knot around the tree with the rope.

Before beginning, instruct participants that where they touch the rope with their right hand must stay connected at that point throughout the activity. They may use their left hand for guidance and this hand may slide along the rope or leave the rope at any time if they wish. You should teach some basic knot tying skills prior to this activity or provide a visual example of a square knot.

2-9 2B or Knot 2B

Welcome to one of my favorite consensus building activities. The spaghetti-like collection of five ropes contains a simple puzzle - which rope holds all the other ropes together?

Invite the members of your group to each find a partner. The initial challenge is for you and your partner to discuss and then agree on which rope you believe connects the other four ropes. Next, see if you can get your entire group to agree. Not too difficult? Well wait, it gets more interesting...

I like to progressively challenge my groups by starting with a rope puzzle that has five different primary colors first, and then proceeding to one with five different striped colors, then onto a puzzle where all five ropes are the same color.

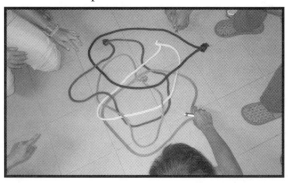

2-10 Disconnected

The tangled ropes for this activity form another consensus building puzzle. You can see a photo of this activity on page 185. For this activity, partners (initially) and the whole group (eventually) are looking for which ropes are NOT connected to any others. Begin with ten different color, texture, diameter and lengths of ropes and connect together in groups of two to four ropes. You can tie rope loops together or knot two or three different ropes together. Then add a final rope that is tied into a loop but disconnected from all other ropes. Next, create a random pile of all these ropes, so it is not easy to spot the rope with the missing connection. Finally, invite your group to solve the puzzle.

There is a significant teachable moment present in this activity.... if we can identify which rope is disconnected from the others in this situation, can we also discover who in our community is disconnected, and help them get connected? Being able to identify missing connections (such as access to helpful resources) is a valuable life skill and one that also builds community within a group.

2-11 Not Knots

Good judgement comes from experience,
and experience comes from bad judgement.

Because of this one activity, I never leave home without a short red rope in my teambuilding kit! In this activity, a 'rope doodle' is constructed and the group is challenged to decide whether this doodle will create a KNOT (please stand to the left side) or NOT A KNOT (move to the right side), when the ends of the rope are pulled. The teachable moment here is to provide the group with tools they can use when group consensus is not easily formed.

Typically, about half of the group thinks the doodle will form a knot and the other half a straight line. Ask participants to partner with a person that has a different viewpoint and try to achieve consensus with them. By considering a different possibility, participants learn to value alternative points of view. The good news is, for this consensus building tool, one of the two people in the group is correct! Then choose a side together, Knot or Not a Knot.

At this point, it is likely that there will still not be a complete consensus within the group. Prior to pulling the ends of the rope, let the members of the group know that you will pull the rope, but slowly, and they can change sides at any time during the unraveling of the knot doodle (this illustrates the ability to make an initial decision, but still be flexible as more information becomes available). It is also a chance to do what John Maxwell refers to as 'failing forward.' Learning from our mistakes improves our future decision making process.

For a significant teachable moment using this activity, see the story *The Value of a Little Red Rope* on page 217 of this book.

2-12 The Missing Link

Here is a consensus puzzle using two different colors of Raccoon Circles. First knot each Raccoon Circle into a loop. You can link these two loops together or leave them separate. Lower these circles to the floor and arrange them so that it is not easy to see whether these two pieces of webbing are LINKED or UNLINKED.

Invite your group to approach and see if they can reach consensus on whether these two circles are linked or not. In a similar technique to Not Knots, invite partnerships to form with members from each side of the argument.

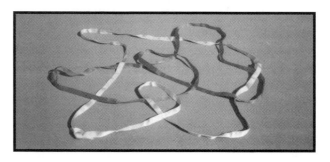

For a higher level of challenge, try this activity using two very long ropes that have each been tied into a circle, or perhaps two ropes that are the same color.

2-13 Stretching the Limit

The challenge for this teambuilding activity is fairly simple - using only the resources currently available to the members of each group, and a few well chosen props from the Rope Games kit, construct the longest continuous line from one location towards another. Group members can use anything now in their possession to construct the longest line (belts, shoelaces, jackets, themselves, etc.).

This activity encourages problem solving, resource management and team commitment. To incorporate a bit of planning into this activity as well, invite teams to brainstorm and prepare for five minutes, following which they'll have one minute to demonstrate their technique. Mark the distance they achieved on their first try. Then after their first attempt, invite them to see if they can invent a way to stretch even farther on their second attempt.

You can also use this activity as a lesson in goal setting. Invite each group to set both a reasonable goal and a 'stretch' goal, and see if they can achieve both in three attempts or less.

2-14 Handcuffs & Shackles

You'll need two soft cotton rope handcuffs with loops at each end for each group of two people. Interlock these rope handcuffs and then invite partners to place a hand in the rope loop at each end of their rope. The challenge is to become disconnected from your partner without untying the knots or removing your hands from the loops in your rope.

As an alternative to working with partners, consider bonding everyone in your group together in a circle and challenging them to separate. This variation often produces a solution that immediately assists the entire team, not just the partners that happen to find the solution quickly.

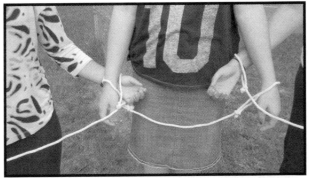

You can also handcuff and shackle a single person to themselves or try turning this kinesthetic challenge into a purely cerebral challenge by connecting the two rope handcuffs through the same opening in a chain link fence.

The solution to all these rope puzzle variations involves passing the middle of your rope handcuffs through the wrist loop of your partner.

2-15 Pot of Gold & Toxic Waste

For this initiative you'll need a long rope knotted into a circle, an additional collection of ropes of various length and a plastic pot (such as a Halloween caldron) that looks like the Pot of Gold at the end of the rainbow. Place the caldron on a small wooden platform (or inverted five gallon bucket) at the center of the rope circle. The challenge is to retrieve the caldron from the center of the circle, using the ropes provided, without anyone or anything touching the ground inside the circle.

A variation of this activity (that uses two containers) is the classic teambuilding activity Toxic Waste. Here the goal is to pick up the full container with an elastic Bull Ring device and transfer the contents to the other container.

For a more creative solution to this challenge, see Thinking Outside the Box on page 132.

2-16 Interference

Here is an extremely loud communication exercise. Begin by dividing your group into three teams. Team One (the senders) occupies the space at the far left of the playing area. Team Two (the receivers) stand to the far right - about 20 feet (6 meters) away. Team Three (the interference) occupies the space in between. Separate each of these teams with an unknotted Raccoon Circle.

Next present Team One with a short message to send to Team Two. Team One members can only verbally or visually convey their message (they cannot relocate or write and pass the message). During this one minute communication period, the members of Team Three try to block (interfere with) the message, by visually and verbally scrambling the information.

After each round, invite teams to change locations (1->2, 2->3, 3->1). After three rounds, debrief the activity and ask teams how they overcame the interference and which role they enjoyed the most and why.

Potential messages include:

In order to listen, you must first become quiet.
The best things in life are not things.
Listen carefully, we have an important message for you.

2-17 All Aboard

You can facilitate a non-platform version of All Aboard by creating an adjustable rope circle. Begin by inviting your group to stand close together and then circle the group with a piece of rope, securing the diameter with a knot. Next, ask your group to stand outside this rope circle and challenge them to reduce the diameter of the circle (by about 25%) and then attempt for everyone to stand within this new perimeter long enough to sing one verse of Row, Row, Row Your Boat. If successful, ask them to create an even smaller circle and try again.

High Tide

This All Aboard variation is designed especially for larger groups. Think of this activity as a beach on a tropical island that keeps getting smaller as the tide comes in. Begin by creating a large rectangle with a long rope. This total area defines the size of the 'beach.' Ask the members of your group to pose for a photo while standing completely within the beach area. Next, inform them that the tide appears to be coming in as you reduce the total area of the beach by shrinking one side of the rectangle. Take another group photo. Continue taking photographs and shrinking the size of the beach until you have effectively reduced the area of the beach to about 20% of the original size. This last position represents high tide and should require some talented problem solving for the group to keep everyone dry on the beach and standing within the limited available space.

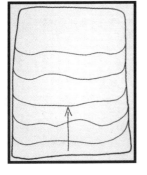

2-18 Photo Finish

Begin this activity by forming a straight rope line. The challenge is for all members of the group to cross this line together. Inform the group that they have fifteen minutes to make five attempts to cross the finish line at exactly the same time. Position yourself so that you can see down the line. Anytime a member of the group crosses the line, even by mistake, yell 'click' to inform them that they have used one of their attempts. Or use a digital camera so that you can show the results of each attempt. Mistakes are common initially, such as someone pointing with their hand or leaning over the line to look at another participant.

This activity involves planning, communication, timing and the ability to deal with frustration. You can further increase the level of challenge by minimizing the space available for planning prior to crossing the finish line.

Thanks to Sam Sikes for sharing this activity.

2-19 Moving Towards Extinction

Create twelve circular rope islands (about the size of a hoola hoop) and spread these randomly around the play area. Do not tie knots in these ropes (which will enable a secondary solution to this challenge). Invite participants to walk (swim) around in the space between these islands. Instruct participants that they are safe from any carnivorous fish in the region anytime they have their feet within the perimeter of an island. Every so often, the facilitator yells "Shark Attack!" and participants flock to reach one of the islands. After each round, one island is removed.

At some point, the available space on the remaining islands will be insufficient for all members of the group, and a breakthrough solution will be necessary for survival. In some cases, participants realize that they only have to have their feet within the perimeter of the island (which is possible while seated around any rope circle). Another unique solution involves participants combining ropes to form larger islands. This secondary solution requires excellent teamwork and problem solving skills.

2-20 Traffic Circle

Traffic Circle uses a single short rope, tied into a circle about 2 feet (0.6 meters) in diameter. This circle is placed at the center of the group. The surprisingly simple task is for each member of the group and their opposite partner to exchange places by passing through the middle of the circle, each touching one body part (foot, hand, nose...) within the rope circle at the same time and then continuing on to stand in the place where their partner began. All this must be accomplished without touching their partner or the rope circle and both participants must be in contact with the ground inside the rope circle at the same time. The group should set a goal to perform this task as quickly as possible.

For a higher level of challenge consider adding a set mousetrap in the center of the traffic circle, or perhaps to exchange the traffic circle entirely with a circle of set mousetraps located in the center of the group. An interesting risk factor here. Be extra careful and wear solid (mousetrap-proof) shoes!

2-21 The Keys to Communication

Begin by dividing your group into two teams standing on opposite sides of a rectangular area created with a long rope. One blindfolded player from each side is invited to sit inside the rectangle. The challenge is for each team to help their blindfolded teammate find specific objects placed inside the rectangular area. Chaos is likely in the first round. Facilitators should stand between the two blindfolded participants to make sure they do not bump into each other.

In round one, simple objects such as keys or tennis balls are used. To complete the challenge, the blindfolded player only needs to locate one of these items and pass it to a player on their team. For each subsequent round the objects get more interesting. In Round Two, two items are needed: a padlock with a matching key (on a keyring for visability). The lock must be opened by the blindfolded player to complete the challenge. Round Three - a combination lock and an index card with the combination written on it (and again, the blindfolded player has to open it, with help from their teammates). Round Four - use your creativity, but consider such things as: crayons and a coloring book or new pencils, sharpeners and an index card on which to write your autograph.

For each round, a new player from each team is selected to be blindfolded. Allow teams a few mintues between each round to discuss their strategy.

This communication activity has many opportunities for discussion and debriefing. Consider some of the following questions:

What communication methods were successful during this activity? What were some of the unsuccessful techniques for communicating with your teammate? What additional suggestions were made but not tried during each round?

2-22 Traffic Jam & People Movers

Use seven rope circles to create the arrangement shown here. Then invite six people to stand in the six outer spaces, leaving the central space unoccupied.

The challenge here is for the three participants on the left to change places with the three on the right. Rules for making this change include that anyone can move forward into an empty space or pass around a member of the other team into an empty space. Participants cannot pass a member of their own team and cannot move backwards. If the group encounters a position from which they cannot complete the task they must return to the beginning and start over.

Try facilitating this task in three stages. In Stage One, the group can talk throughout the task. In Stage Two, they must complete the task without talking (which verifies that they have a workable plan). In Stage Three, they must complete the task without breathing! That is, they must each take a deep breath and complete the task before anyone needs to take another breath (typically about 20 seconds).

Traffic Jam requires a minimum of 15 moves to complete.

People Movers

Here are two more challenges modeled after wooden peg shuttle puzzles that you can create with rope circles. For the M puzzle, no jumping is allowed only sliding into an open space. Players can slide any number of spaces in one turn as long as they only slide through open spaces and along the lines connecting each location. The challenge is for the team of four on the left side to change places with the team of four on the right side.

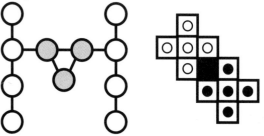

Our final People Mover challenge requires ten people. The challenge is for the five people inhabiting the black dot locations to trade places with the five people in the white dot locations. Moves include sliding into an open space (such as the black square in the middle) and jumping over any other player on the board, including a member of your own team.

2-23 The Longest Line

This activity incorporates both a treasure hunt and some creative problem solving. Begin with a ball of common packaging string. Cut a hundred or more small pieces, varying in length from 5 to 10 inches (13 - 25cm). Next, scatter these small pieces of string within a well defined space, such as a gymnasium, conference room, classroom, cafeteria, basketball court or playing field. Place a few pieces of string in places that are easy to find and half or more in more challenging locations, such as sticking out of the pages of a closed book or partially concealed beneath a coffee mug.

   The challenge is for teams to collect as many of these small pieces of string as possible within a short time period. Next they need to knot all the various pieces of string together. The team with The Longest Line wins!

   For this activity, knot tying skills are equally important to the speed of recovering as many pieces of string as possible within the time limit. A knot that is both strong and requires minimal string to create is a good choice.

2-24 10 x 10 x 10

Here is one of my favorite leadership activities. The title of this activity comes from the challenge - a chosen leader has ten minutes to get ten people to traverse a space ten feet wide. The mode of transportation is several 'walking boards' constructed from 1/2 inch (12 mm) thick plywood squares (12" x 12") with flat climbing webbing handles (60 inches / 1.5 meters long) attached to each board. Additional team members are invited to be silent observers.

Begin this challenge with ten people standing on eleven walking boards that have been placed in a U configuration. Each person initially

82

stands with each foot on a different board. Select one person as the leader and give them the task of 'getting the job done.' Then start the clock.

In the space behind the starting line, the group can plan and experiment with different techniques. But once anyone crosses over the starting line, only the walking boards can touch the ground. Only the people who cross the starting line on any particular walking board are allowed to touch that board during the completion of the task. Planning time is part of the 10 minutes. Only one person is allowed to hold the rope extending upward from any walking board.

There are many opportunities for teachable moments and leadership evaluation from 10x10x10. One of the most common mistakes is that the leader assumes the rules don't apply to them (specifically with regards to not touching the ground between the two ropes).

Other reviewing topics include a discussion of how the 10 minutes were used. Was there a plan in place before the first person crossed the starting line? Did the plan change during the completion of the task? Were ideas given an adequate chance to be explained and tried? Did the leader complete the task successfully? Were the rules properly followed throughout the activity? What skills did you learn during the completion of this task?

Just Passing Through

The next seven activities in this chapter involve the members of a group passing through a variety of openings made of rope. Each activity is slightly different. The Worm Hole for example, is a very portable version of the Spider Web initiative, handy when you happen to be in a location without trees. The Electric Box is a wonderful activity for discussing adapting to change. Inside / Out brings with it a discussion on ethical behavior in the workplace.

Here you will find variations of webs, windows, doorways and other openings made of rope. Successfully passing through these challenging openings requires teamwork, communication and attention to the smallest details. Some challenges involve support from other team members. Always lift and transfer fellow team members carefully and safely. Anyone passing through an opening should always be in contact with at least one other team member at all times. Good luck, be safe and don't forget to discuss the teachable moments that occur along the way.

2-25 Spider Web Variations

Here are a few of my favorite variations of the Spider Web and Electric Fence initiatives. For each of these activities, I like to begin with half of the group on each side of the obstacle. This insures adequate spotting on each side. When possible and practical, I like to give the group a roll of string and have them create the web themselves, with a sufficient number of holes for each member of the group.

The traditional Spider Web is a vertical web, with openings ranging from big to small. The challenge is for every team member to pass through the web, assisted by their teammates, without anyone touching the web. Careful spotting is necessary when lifting and transporting any member of the group.

The Electric Fence (see illustration on page 88) requires two elastic ropes. The goal is to pass each member of the group to the other side with 1/3 of the group going over the upper rope, 1/3 through the middle between the ropes, and 1/3 going underneath the lower rope. Spotting is required for this activity.

The Horizontal Spider Web requires a group to traverse the web, from one side to the opposite, without touching the web. Objects can be placed within an opening and collected by the group if they pass through that opening.

If you would like to use a vertical Spider Web for an activity that does not require transporting people, see how fast you can pass a single tennis ball through each of the available openings, without touching the web or dropping the ball.

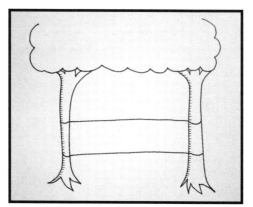

The Electric Fence & Over the Fence

2-26 Over the Fence

Here is a portable version of the Electric Fence. Begin with two participants holding a knotted Raccoon Circle, with the long parallel sides about 12 inches apart. Place half of the group on each side of this Raccoon Circle "fence." The first two persons (one from each side) pass over the fence (one at a time) with the fence 6 inches above the ground. The next two persons have the height increased to 12 inches above the ground, and so on.

This Raccoon Circle version of the Electric Fence places an equal number of spotters on both sides of the fence at all times. It also provides a changing level of challenge to the group. Even at the lowest levels, it is required that all participants crossing the fence be in contact with at least two other participants at all times during the crossing. Allowing two participants to hold the Raccoon Circle also leaves an opportunity for those that choose not to be transported. Or, if the holders do wish to pass over the fence, they can trade places with other team members during the event.

Allow adequate time for teams to plan which group members will be transported at each of the various levels.

2-27 The Worm Hole

The Worm Hole is an elastic circle made from shock (bungie) cord. The challenge is for the entire team to pass through the Worm Hole to the 'other side.' Worm Holes are dangerous places in space, so when you travel through one, you want to be in constant contact with a partner throughout the journey. You cannot touch the Worm Hole as you pass through, but other group members can hold the Worm Hole open for you. Once someone has held the Worm Hole and then let go, they cannot hold it again.

For an additional challenge, every group of partners passing through the Worm Hole should do so in a different manner. Or, some groups could carry something along with them. The rules say that no one can touch the Worm Hole as they pass through, however touching the hand of a holder while passing through is acceptable and occasionally necessary.

2-28 The Window of Opportunity

For this activity, a vertical window is created by two people holding a knotted Raccoon Circle or by supporting a Raccoon Circle between two trees. The challenge is for each half of the group (standing on opposite sides) to transfer through the Window of Opportunity without touching the Raccoon Circle. You can create a single window size for all members of the group, randomly change the size of the window throughout the activity, or allow individuals to create their own window size, shape and height above the floor.

Modifying the size of the window is an excellent metaphor for change. Planning also becomes important, so that each participant passes through the Window of Opportunity at the optimal time for their abilities, talents and size.

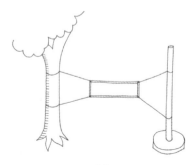

2-29 The Electric Box

*It is not the strongest of the species
that survives, nor the most intelligent,
but the one most responsive to change.*
                                    Charles Darwin

The changing shape of the Electric Box requires
some advanced planning and strategy. The box,
made of a single knotted Raccoon Circle, begins
as a horizontal rectangle and constantly changes
so that no two people ever move through the
same geometrical opening. The challenge is for
each person in the group to pass through, without
touching the Raccoon Circle.

For each participant passing through The
Electric Box, the box changes shape, providing
everyone with a new and unique challenge.
Spencer Johnson wrote about exactly this process
in his book, *Who Moved My Cheese?* The one
constant in our lives is that things change.

Thanks to Patrick Caton for sharing this activity.

2-30 Circle the Circle

This activity and Human Knot (from Chapter 4 of this book) are two of the first teambuilding activities I ever experienced in my youth.

Circle the Circle invites a circle of participants to join hands. A hoola hoop or knotted Raccoon Circle loop are then added to the circle. The challenge is to pass this loop or hoop completely around the circle as quickly and carefully as possible. See photo on page 94.

Once this initial and fairly easy challenge has been accomplished, raise the stakes by passing one loop to the left and a second loop to the right around the circle, at the same time.

Large diameter hoola hoops work fine for this activity. The more flexible Raccoon Circles also work, but require an even higher level of skill. As a final challenge, tie a Raccoon Circle into a figure 8 configuration, passing the upper loop to the left and the lower loop to the right at the same time. This configuration requires a significant level of teamwork, problem solving and patience as well as some increased agility due to the smaller loop sizes.

Circle the Circle and Inside / Out

2-31 Inside / Out

Here is an activity that explores ethical behavior. Begin by providing each group of eight people with a knotted Raccoon Circle placed on the floor. Invite them to step inside. The challenge is for the entire group to exit the circle by passing underneath the Raccoon Circle without using their arms or shoulders or hands. Encourage the group to leave the circle and hold an 'offsite planning meeting' nearby. Then invite them to return and carry out their plan.

Most groups easily complete the task, but typically interpret the rules to mean that they cannot touch the rope with their arms, shoulders or hands. Many participants use their hands to balance or as they crawl on their hands and knees to exit (see photo on previous page). This common result can lead to an interesting discussion on following rules as well as the integrity of the group. Additional reviewing can include a discussion about the initial plan and whether it was followed or modified during the completion of the task. To assess whether on not your group has learned a valuable lesson in this activity, ask them to repeat the process, but this time from the outside in. See if they repeat the offsite planning phase or jump right into the task and watch if they correct the errors from their first attempt.

2-32 On Target

The challenge of this activity is for a blindfolded quarterback to successfully throw an array of objects through a rope loop target held by other team members. The distance thrown can change from ten to fifty feet (3-15 meters). The items thrown can change from tennis balls to beachballs to water balloons to flying discs to paper airplanes to rubber chickens. The diameter of the target rope loop held by the team can change from two to five feet (0.6-1.5 meters).

As shown in this illustration, you'll need a knotted Raccoon Circle for the quarterback to stand in, a long boundary rope for setting the distance and a second knotted Raccoon Circle for the target team. Encourage the target team members and quarterback to communicate with each other, and occasionally invite them to change roles as well.

2-33 Blind Find

It occurs to me that at the core of many teambuilding activities is an inefficient process. And that process is what makes the activity interesting. So it is with this communication activity. The goal here is for small teams to find an object located somewhere in front of them.

Each team consists of three players: a sightless or blindfolded searcher, a sightless or blindfolded communicator, and a speechless spotter. The spotter and communicator work out a system for directional information (tapping on shoulders for example to communicate left, right, forward, back). Based upon the information provided by the mute spotter, the communicator tells the searcher where to look. The object to be found can be any one of the items in the Rope Games kit, from a small rope 'worm' to the full length rope.

2-34 Cross the Line

Here is an excellent opportunity to discuss conflict, negotiation and win/win, win/lose and lose/lose scenarios. To begin, invite participants to find partners of approximately the same physical size and to stand on opposite sides of a rope line between them.

Begin the activity by having the partner on one side of the line say the following phrase:

There ain't no flies on me.
There ain't no flies on me.
There might be flies on you,
but there ain't no flies on me.

Then instruct the other side to repeat this phrase. Next ask the first partner to step closer to the line and repeat the phrase with twice the energy. Finally the second partner also steps closer and repeats the phrase with twice the energy. At this point, the facilitator says, "you have five seconds to get that person on your side of the line. Go!"

Typically, the phrasing and urgency of the challenge results in a rather quick tug of war between partners, and usually a physical resolution to the challenge. Leaving open a major opportunity to discuss conflict, challenge, attitude, negotiation, and how to resolve differences between people.

Safety Note: During this activity, some participants may try to pull their opponent over to their side. Be sure your audience knows of the physical nature of this activity before the challenge begins.

2-35 Rock Around the Clock

Begin by inviting participants to stand around a rope circle, with their feet touching their neighbor's feet.

The challenge here is for the person in the 12 o'clock position (where the knot is located) to rotate clockwise around the circle to the 6 o'clock position, moving everyone else in the process, without anyone loosing contact with their neighbor's feet.

Additional contact (such as holding hands) is optional, but a good problem solving technique. This is one of those 'easy to present - difficult to perform' challenges. If the group experiences difficulty, invite them to have a seat on the floor, place their feet in contact with their neighbor and brainstorm a solution from this position. Groups quickly discover that it is easier to complete the challenge from a seated position, compared to their initial standing position.

Debriefing questions include: Why didn't the group consider the sitting position solution earlier? Did participants call out their own mistakes, or did they try to hide them?

2-36 Alphabet Soup

For this fast paced problem solving and goal setting activity, you'll need twenty-six index cards with the letters A through Z, placed face up, in random order in a large rope circle, an unknotted Raccoon Circle about 20 feet away for the start/finish line and a stopwatch.

The challenge of this activity is for each of the cards to be touched one at a time, in alphabetical order, with not more than one person within the perimeter of the circle at any time.

Before beginning each round, invite teams to establish a time goal. Time begins when the first person crosses the starting line and ends when the last person crosses the finish line. When each round is completed, compare the estimate to the actual performance. Errors, such as touching a card out of order, touching the perimeter rope or having more than one person within the perimeter of the circle at the same time, carry a five second penalty for each occurrence. Many groups experience quite a few errors initially but tend to improve with each new trial.

2-37 Match Cards

This version of the memory game begins by selecting twelve different words from the subject matter you wish to explore and placing each word on two different index cards. Shuffle these cards and place them face down in a 4x6 grid. Create several decks of these cards, break your next group into smaller teams, and you'll have a competitive activity that increases the energy of the group and can educate them as well.

Place an unknotted Raccoon Circle starting line on the floor for each team and place their cards ten feet beyond the line. One person from each team can cross the line and turn over two cards. If they match, they stay in the same location face up. If they don't match, this player turns them face down and returns. The first team to turn over all twenty-four cards wins. But the real value of this activity is that after completing the task, the cards that were used for the activity become the tools used in the debriefing and reviewing process.

For the first level of reviewing, invite each person to take one card that contains a word they feel is important and tell the group why they chose this card. Next, ask the group to select from these twelve words their top five most imporant words. A discussion on the value of each word typically occurs. Finally, ask the group which one word they would like to focus on for the remainder of the program.

For even more activities with index cards, watch for the new book *It's all in the Cards* by Jim Cain (www.teamworkandteamplay.com)

2-38 Minefield & Lighthouse

My favorite way to facilitate The Minefield is to outline a square area with a long rope and fill that space with random soft objects such as short pieces of rope. Next, invite everyone to find a partner. Blindfold one partner standing near the rope. Their sighted partner then stands on the opposite side of the square and gives them verbal commands to help them navigate the minefield without touching any of the objects.

A second, less 'explosive' metaphor is called Lighthouse. In this version, one person is the ship. They attempt to navigate the rocky coastline waters (with their eyes closed). Their partner plays the role of lighthouse (eyes open) and provides verbal information to help the ship navigate. The goal is for the lighthouse to help their ship reach port safely while navigating the debris-laden waters.

To make the process a bit more challenging in each version, all blindfolded partners are placed in the same space, at the same time and must navigate around not only the debris but all the other participants as well. If a blindfolded participant touches anything during their crossing, such as an object on the ground or another participant within the region, they must return to their original starting position and try again. After a successful crossing, partners are invited to switch roles.

2-39 Reaching for Your Goals

For this activity you'll need one index card for each participant and one knotted Raccoon Circle for each group of six to eight people.

Invite each person to write down a personal or professional goal they have. Next, have them place this index card on the floor one full stride outside the perimeter of the Raccoon Circle. Then have groups gather within their respective Raccoon Circles. Invite each person to share their goal with their group, and then, using only themselves and the others in the group, attempt to retrieve their goal card without touching the ground outside the Raccoon Circle. In this case, the metaphor of having your teammates help you achieve your goals is profound. Many of the goals we set for ourselves could use a little outside help.

2-40 Shape Up

I recommend this kinesthetic teambuilding activity especially for children. Start by providing each group of six with a knotted Raccoon Circle. Next, challenge them to create letters, numbers and shapes using their Raccoon Circle. Make sure everyone has at least one hand on the circle at all times.

Start with fairly simple items, such as the letter O, D or P, followed by more challenging ones, such as the number 4 and the letter R. Next, move into some standard two dimensional shapes, like a square, triangle or house. Then move on to three dimensional shapes, such as a four-legged household pet (and you must provide a name), a jet airplane or a pyramid.

2-41 A Knot Between Us

This rope activity can be a bit more challenging than expected. Begin by providing a short length (about 6 feet or 2 meters) of rope between each person in a line of six (you'll need a total of five ropes). Ask these participants to maintain their grip on their end of the rope for the duration of the activity. Next, challenge them to create a single overhand knot on each of the five ropes. The physical gyrations required to tie just a single knot are significant. Five knots will take even more effort.

When complete, challenge the group to reverse the process and remove each knot.

2-42 Knot Our Problem

Rope knots can be helpful when holding things together or harmful when the ropes become tangled. This activity explores all kinds of knots.

Begin by pre-knotting a collection of rope or webbing segments and inviting each group to select one that represents the kind of challenges they are presently dealing with on a daily basis. Then challenge them to remove all the knots. Discuss what needed to happen to remove the harmful knots (addiction, social problems, lack of resources, dysfunction). Also discuss how to keep the helpful knots in our lives (connection to family, friends, resources).

For your pre-knotted rope collection, use a wide variety of rope, webbing and cordage of all kinds, different styles of knots and significantly different difficulties. I used a 10,000 psi hydraulic press to knot a few of them. I don't think those knots will be coming out any time soon!

For a more playful version of this activity, see the game Frozen Knots in Chapter Six. And just to illustrate how such activities can work in real life, consider the story on the next page.

A Story About Knots

We had been working with a group of 13 & 14 year old girls. They were all struggling with issues (you know, the kind of stuff that breaks your heart). We had just completed a check-in with them. Clearly it had been a rough day for most of them and they had so much on their minds. We decided to use the activity Knot Our Problem. We used the analogy of the Raccoon Circle as the road of life, where the knots signified the bumps in the road or the problems they were facing. We invited each girl to name their knot (problem) and then to work collectively to untie them. This was such an incredible experience! When we processed after the initiative, the girls candidly discussed their behaviors. They learned so much about themselves and working together. One girl really needed help, but found it hard to ask. One was thrilled that the girls helped her even when she didn't ask. Another girl noticed that she kind of sat back and let the other girls untie her knot (solve her problems). And yet another girl noticed that sometimes well meaning friends try to help you out and actually make things worse. This was truly the right initiative at the right time with the right group!

Jennifer Steinmetz
Rocky Top Therapy Center

2-43 Tossing Pizza

While playfully simple, this Raccoon Circle activity teaches some basic principles of problem solving, communication and teamwork.

Begin by providing each group of six to eight people with one knotted Raccoon Circle. Inform them of the rules for this year's pizza tossing championship. They are to toss their Raccoon Circle pizza high into the air and have everyone in their group catch it, with no one moving their feet. Everyone needs to be initially touching the circle, palms up, elbows straight, with no slack in the circle. Allow groups a few minutes to practice. A good pizza tossing team can succeed at this task three times in a row!

For a higher level of challenge, encourage groups to not only toss their pizza into the air, but to spin it just as the best pizza chefs do in Italy. It turns out that a little spin can actually improve the team's performance. You might even challenge one team to toss their Raccoon Circle pizza so that another team can catch it.

2-44 The Chain Gang

Begin with the entire team standing single file in a line. Next, place a long rope on the right shoulder of each person. The goal of the group is to see how far they can walk, without allowing the rope to touch the ground or slide off of their shoulders or to be touched with their arms or hands. For most groups, the rope will sway, slide and eventually fall off. After the first failure, invite the team to brainstorm ideas for improvement (such as standing on opposite sides of the rope). For safety reasons, only place the rope upon participants' shoulders, NEVER around their necks.

2-45 Jumping Rope

The challenge of this activity is for the entire group to pass through the turning rope without touching or stopping the rope. Two volunteers are asked to turn the rope. Here are a few possibilities for transit in order of increasing difficulty.

Option 1 - Individuals can go at any time, in any number. This is the ideal 'first time' mode.
Option 2 - Each time the rope turns, one individual must pass through.
Option 3 - Each time the rope turns, pairs must pass through.
Option 4 - Each time the rope turns, groups of four must pass through.
Option 5 - repeat Options 1-4, but instead of passing through, everyone must jump the rope exactly once.

*There are dozens of books, websites and ideas for rope jumping, including double dutch, solo jumping, team jumping, cardio workouts and much, much more. One free resources for rope games is the Toronto Public Health Department – Go Play Rope Games – www.toronto.ca/health.

2-46 The Clock

This Raccoon Circle activity is especially useful with young children. Now you have a kinesthetic method for teaching children how to tell time!

Begin by providing groups of eight with a knotted Raccoon Circle. Ask them to rotate so that the water knot on the Raccoon Circle is pointed directly at the facilitator. This is the position for 12 o'clock midnight. Inform the group that you are going to shout out a specific time and their job is to quickly move their feet (not their hands) and rotate the position of the knot on their Raccoon Circle to coincide with the position of the hour hand on a clock.

Ready? Here we go.... 3am, 7am, 9:30am, 9:25am (no, clocks can't move backwards!), twelve noon, 1:57pm, 4:43pm, dinnertime, 8pm, bedtime, 11:59pm, midnight (and all is well).

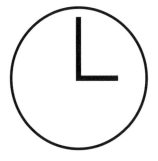

2-47 Line Up

Line Up is a linear teambuilding activity that requires some creative forms of communication. Place a long, straight piece of rope on the ground and then ask the members of your group to line up according to the criteria below. When the group has finished, perform a quick quality control check by asking each person in line to share their contribution with the group.

Line Up by birthday, from January 1st to December 31st, without talking. In groups of twenty-three people, there is a 50% chance that two people will share the same birthday! With 57 people, that percentage grows to 99%!

Line Up by height, from tallest to shortest, with your eyes closed. What is the combined height of the entire group?

Line Up alphabetically by the first letter of your middle name, without saying that letter or name.

Line Up by number of years of service in this organization, without talking and with your hands behind your back.

Line Up by the last digit of your telephone number without talking or using your hands.

2-48 Spiral Labyrinth

Here is a communication activity for partners. One blindfolded partner navigates a Spiral Labyrinth they have not seen. A sighted partner provides information to assist them through the labyrinth. The labyrinth can be created with a long rope or masking tape. At the center of the labyrinth might be a treasure, an object to retrieve or a different exit path.

For additional challenge, the blindfolded partner might be asked to transport a bucket of water, perform a task along the way, or occasionally take a step on their own without guidance from their sighted partner.

2-49 A Work of Art

For this artistic communication activity you'll need two identical sets of props. These can include ropes from the Rope Games kit plus anything else you can find in pairs nearby (water bottles, shoes, hats, books, etc.)

The challenge is for one group of artists to use these props to create something artistic and for the other group (the replicators) to reproduce this design. Once the artists have completed their task, one member of each group meets in a neutral location (where neither can see their artwork) and one minute is allotted for them to share information about their artwork. These participants then rejoin their groups, work for another minute, and then a second pair meets to discuss their work. This continues for six meetings after which the replicators have two additional minutes to complete their design. When the replicators have finished, the two groups are allowed to see each other's artwork. For simplicity, it can be helpful to place each piece of artwork on a tarp or plywood, so that when finished, the two pieces of artwork can be brought together and analyzed side by side.

2-50 Yurt Circle Balance

You'll need one knotted Raccoon Circle for each group of eight. Begin by inviting participants to grasp the Raccoon Circle with their hands and feet about shoulder width apart. Then invite teams to lean back slightly and balance the circle.

Next, ask participants to bend their knees, lean back and slowly lower the circle to almost a sitting position and then raise the circle and return to a standing position. You can invite groups to make one sound while going down and a different sound when standing up.

The dynamic balance required to perform this activity is a useful metaphor for working together as a team.

2-51 Jump the River

Here are two variations of the same activity. As a physical challenge and a potential warm up activity, invite the members of your group to jump a river, made from two long ropes, parallel to each other. Begin with ropes that are about 3 feet (1 meter) apart. Increase the width of the river after each round. Continue until more team members are splashing into the river than successfully jumping over it.

Version two allows for some helpful teamwork. Place two long ropes in a V pattern. Invite team members to stand at the location they believe they can successfully cross without landing in the water. Now ask them to take two steps sideways towards a wider section of the river. Invite the group to brainstorm how to get everyone successfully over the river.

One potential solution is to have two helpful spotters provide additional lift to the person crossing the river. The rules only say that the person crossing cannot touch the water. In this case, teamwork makes what might seem impossible, possible!

2-52 Shoelaces

Here is a teambuilding challenge for partners wearing shoes with laces. Ask one person in each group to untie their shoelaces. Next, with each partner supplying one hand, ask them to work together to re-tie the shoelaces.

After the first attempt, ask them to repeat the process, this time using their non-dominant hands. Finally, ask them to repeat the process again, but this time with their eyes closed.

Partners will need communication, problem solving skills and teamwork to succeed in this task.

Thanks to Jennifer Stanchfield for sharing this activity.

Some Thoughts About Trust Activities

One of the trust activities most often portrayed in television programs, at best as silly and at worst as dangerous, is the trust fall initiative. At the time of writing this book, I know of at least one current lawsuit stemming from a participant's inclusion in a less-than-successful trust fall.

Simply stated, the risk-benefit ratio of the trust fall initiative is wrong. Too high a risk for the limited benefit provided. In as many ways as possible I have attempted to illustrate alternative ways of building trust through physical activities in this book. I would gladly replace the trust fall with any of the following activities, including my preferred concluding trust activity, The Trust Lift, which can be found on page 122.

When attempting to build trust between the members of a group, it is essential to choose activities which maximize the potential for success and minimize the potential for error.

Be safe, and give some serious thought to replacing the high risk trust fall activity with another, less risky, equally valuable and more suitable alternative.

2-53 The Tight Rope Walker

Here is a fun activity that encourages spotting practice. A slackline or circus high wire is replaced by a long string or rope at ground level. One participant at a time traverses this rope line, with multiple spotters on each side. At any moment, they may need the support and spotting of their group members, who remain in ready spotting position throughout this activity.

As they begin, they may travel a few steps confidently and then find their legs intentionally wobbling before dramatically leaning to one side (and being caught by spotters), only to be righted and then tilted to the other side. The most important element of this activity is for spotters to be ever vigilent and ready to catch their partner at any moment. Carefully observe the spotters in this activity, and offer suggestions and recommendations for improvement where appropriate.

121

2-54 Trust Lift

The Trust Lift can be a meaningful way to complete a trust sequence with a group. Here, eight team members carefully lift one of their teammates. While this can be done with hands only, I prefer the Raccoon Circle approach because it provides excellent support. It is also useful in colder months when slippery jackets make lifting by hand difficult.

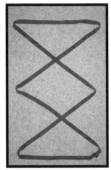

To begin, create a double hourglass shape with a knotted Raccoon Circle. This shape provides handholds for six lifters and a supportive cradle for the person being lifted.

Invite a volunteer to lie down upon the Raccoon Circle, face up, so that their feet extend below the cradle, and their shoulder blades are even with the top edge. Three lifters are stationed on each side of the person: at the position of their shoulders, waist and knees. An additional spotter is located at the head, and is responsible for the head, neck and shoulder region of the person being lifted (the most critical spotting location). A final spotter is located at the feet of the person being lifted and is charged with keeping the feet and head at the same elevation throughout the Trust Lift.

The head spotter now invites the other lifters to join them and lift the person to waist height in one smooth motion. The head spotter is in a perfect position to observe each of the lifters and to remind them keep their backs straight and lift properly. This same head spotter is also in position to verbally reassure the person being lifted, *"no worries, we have you, you are doing fine."*

If the participant and lifters wish, the participant can continue to be lifted up to shoulder level and then slowly lowered back to ground level as the cradle is gently rocked back and forth (from head to foot) in a relaxing descent. When the participant reaches ground level, the members of the lifting square are invited to gently press this person into the ground, to reattach them with the earth. Tom Smith would say that after flying with the eagles, you need to be sure you are re-connected to the earth!

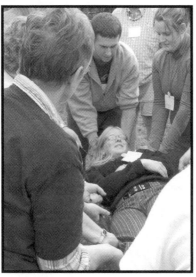

While the explanation described here uses a Raccoon Circle for the Trust Lift, additional facilitator intervention is necessary for a safe and successful trust lift. Appropriate spotting techniques are essential for this activity. If you are not experienced in safely facilitating this and other trust activities in this book, DO NOT ATTEMPT THEM!

2-55 Trust Walk

You can use a long rope as a connection tool for your next group trust walk. To maintain spacing between participants, tie an overhand knot for each person along the rope to give them a tactile reminder of their position. Group members are encouraged to keep their eyes closed during this activity. Sighted facilitators should be placed at the beginning and end of the rope. Avoid steep inclines, staircases and other safety concerns but look for interesting opportunities, such as walking from sunlight into shade or changing textures of pavement and grass.

2-56 The Maze

The Maze is a large-scale labyrinth created with several hundred feet of rope or string and a suitable grove of trees. After creating the maze, lead a blindfolded team into the center of the maze, invite them to grasp the rope in their hands, and challenge them to find the exit.

For safety reasons, no member of the group is allowed to step over or pass under the rope. Participants are encouraged to keep one hand on the rope at all times. While in the maze, communication is encouraged, but upon reaching the exit, talking is no longer allowed. The facilitator will quietly inform participants when they have reached the exit.

One of the first questions often voiced by a group is whether to stay together or separate to find the exit.

2-57 London Bridge

Two ropes are placed 10 feet apart to designate the banks of a river. Half the members of the group are placed on each side. Additional props include a long and strong rope (such as a climbing rope or large diameter tug-of-war rope) and two hardwood (oak) dowels 1.5 inches in diameter and 40 inches long.

The challenge is to create a system that will transport at least one (and perhaps all) of the members from each side of the river safely to the other side without touching the river. Crawling along the rope is difficult and should be discouraged. One potential technique involves wrapping the long rope multiple times around each dowel and pulling the rope taught. Team members hold onto the dowels and the tail ends of the rope. One person grasps the middle of the rope (with their hands and legs) and both teams lift and then walk in the same direction to transfer this person over the river to the other side.

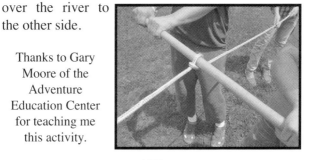

Thanks to Gary Moore of the Adventure Education Center for teaching me this activity.

127

2-58 Twins

Imagine a rope version of the activity Alphabet Soup (Number 2-36 in this chapter) or a timed scavenger hunt and you have a pretty good idea what Twins is all about. Start with a random collection of small pieces of rope, string, webbing and other forms of cordage. You'll need two pieces that are exactly the same (twins) for each sample. Place one of each sample into a pile at the center of a rope circle and give each of the other twins to the members of the group (one piece per person).

The challenge is for the entire group to find the twin to their piece of rope as quickly as possible. Only one person can be within the perimeter of the rope circle at a time. Time begins when the first person enters the circle and concludes when the last person exits (provided that everyone has found their true twin). Each group has three attempts to achieve their best time.

In round two, there are still a variety of cordage lengths, diameters, textures, styles and sizes, but all of the rope segments are the same color.

In the final round, each of the pieces of rope are from the same stock, so that only minor changes in length or pattern or perhaps a few well placed knots, can be used to tell various pieces apart.

2-59 If You Need Help, Just Raise Your Hand

Here is an interesting challenge with a unique solution that works well with medium to large groups. Create a rope circle by knotting the ends of a long rope together and ask ten team members to hold the rope waist high from the outside of the circle. Next ask the remaining members of the group to stand inside the rope circle with their eyes closed. The challenge is then explained:

The goal is to reach the outside of the circle. You cannot go under the circle. You cannot go over the circle. You cannot touch the rope. You cannot untie the knot. If you need help, just raise your hand.

While the challenge can seem a bit confusing and difficult, the solution is actually presented in the information above. If you need help, just raise your hand. All those raising their hands are silently assisted by one of the external members of the team to the outside of the circle.

It can be helpful to tell the remaining members of the group when a participant has successfully made it to the outside of the circle. It is ok, and in this case appropriate, to ask for help.

2-60 Exit Strategy

Instruct the members of your group to stand around the perimeter of a large rope circle. Invite one third of the group to stand inside the circle, eyes closed, bending at the waist and grasping their ankles. The remaining members of the group joins hands around the circle, except at one location (which is the exit).

The members of the inside group are instructed to find the exit of the circle and communicate this information to their teammates. But there are several things that make this process a bit more challenging. First, players inside the circle must always be grasping their ankles, eyes closed, and they can only move backwards. Second, these same players can only communicate by saying a single nonsense word (such as 'quack'). And third, the location of the exit can move several times during the course of the activity.

Once players inside the circle pass through the exit they may open their eyes (but they are still required to grasp their ankles, walk backwards and communicate with only one word).

2-61 Linearity

Here is a visual challenge that is part puzzle, part consensus-building activity. You'll need two ropes cut from the same stock. One 6 feet (2 meters) long and the second 3 feet (1 meter) long. You'll also need a wooden board or a piece of thick cardboard to cover the mid-section of the longest rope.

The challenge is for a group to collectively decide which of the two rope ends on the right side of this puzzle is connected to the rope that appears on the left. The path of the continuous rope is guaranteed to be a straight line. Group members are welcome to utilize any available tools, such as tape measures, straight-edges or perhaps a 2x4 piece of lumber or another piece of rope. The wooden board can only be removed once consensus has been reached.

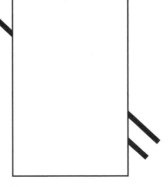

2-62 Thinking Outside the Box

It may seem that there are insufficient resources to accomplish this next task, but in reality, the greatest resource is always the creativity of the group themselves!

With a long rope, create a large square and place an object at the center. The group challenge is to retrieve the object without anyone touching the ground inside the square.

There are several interesting solutions to this challenge. Some groups may use resources they currently possess (shoelaces, belts, etc.) to fabricate a lifting device to remove the object. But there are even more elegant solutions possible. One of the most creative solutions I've seen is for the group to transform the square into a circle and then simply walk into the circle and remove the object as a team. Another 'out of the box' solution is to kick the rope square closer and closer to the object, and then reach over the rope and remove the object without touching the ground inside the square.

If you want to promote this kind of Thinking Outside the Box, see my comments on the following page.

A Few Words About Group Creativity

One of the most fascinating elements of many adventure-based activities is that there can be multiple solutions to a challenge. I would encourage facilitators to be open to new and novel solutions to any activity. Nothing, in my opinion, is worse than asking a group to be creative and then not accepting a truly outside the box approach they suggest or imposing additional constraints so that their innovative suggestion becomes impractical. Obviously there is the need for physical and emotional safety, and these guidelines should be taken into consideration at all times. But if a group suggests a really innovative solution to a challenge, and it meets the necessary guidelines, including safety, congratulate them and invite them to demonstrate their recommended method.

Once, when I was using the Work of Art activity with a group, the replicated artwork was nearly an identical reproduction of the orginal. When I complimented the group on their excellent communication capabilities, one team member showed me the photo he had taken with his cell phone and then texted to a person in the other half of the group. My goal was to improve communication between these two groups and using the tools they had at hand, they did. Well done!

2-63 Bull Ring Variations

Bull Ring is one of the simplest teambuilding tools ever. In addition to the versions shared earlier in this chapter, here are a few more variations that you can try. For starters, you can replace the metal ring with a flexible chain (higher difficulty), plastic platform (an inverted flying disc), a pair of wooden salad tong scissors (to pick things up) or a giant paint brush so the group can write one calligraphy character of significance.

On this page you'll find Human Bull Ring (made from a plywood disk and heavy duty climbing ropes), the Tower of Power (wooden blocks and a lifting mechanism - www.metalog. co.uk), an elastic ring version (perfect for the activity Toxic Waste or for creating a pyramid by stacking six plastic cups) and a makeshift version made from carabiners and ropes.

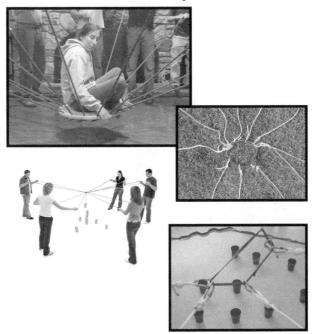

Shown here is another version of Write On! from Europe and a final version from New England, where the pen is stationary and the team moves the paper (on a wooden platform) beneath it.

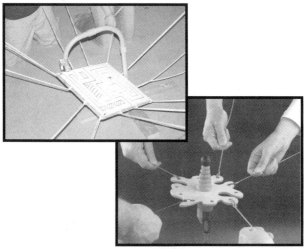

And finally, one last Bull Ring idea. Attach a short string and tennis ball to a regular Bull Ring to create a Bull Ring Pendulum. The challenge with this tool is to knock over 10 plastic bowling pins as quickly as possible. While some groups may repeatedly swing the Tennis Ball Pendulum to knock over one pin at a time, a quicker technique is to drop the entire apparatus to almost ground level and pull over all the bowling pins at once!

Chapter Three
Tricks, Stunts, Puzzles & Other Challenges

This chapter contains tricks and puzzles with which you can amuse your audience.

No.	Name	Category	Group Size
3-1	Houses & Utilities	Puzzle	Small
3-2	Sliders	Puzzle	Small
3-3	Make a Knot	Puzzle	Any
3-4	15th Object	Puzzle	Small
3-5	Pencil Pushers	Physical	Foursomes
3-6	That's My Hat	Physical	Trios
3-7	Smell the Rope	Trick	Small
3-8	Erasable Knots	Puzzle	Small
3-9	Chefalo Knot	Puzzle	Small
3-10	BLW Puzzle	Puzzle	Any
3-11	Buttonholer	Puzzle	Any
3-12	Pigs & Pens	Puzzle	Small
3-13	Silent Bells	Puzzle	Partners
3-14	Line Drawings	Puzzle	Small
3-15	Five Rooms	Puzzle	Small
3-16	Jump Rope	Challenge	Small

3-1 Houses & Utilities

This classic puzzle has been around for more than a century and still baffles folks. Trade in the pencil and paper version for the cardboard and rope version shown here. You'll need nine ropes and six cardboard cutouts for the houses and utilities. Arrange the six cardboard cutouts as shown.

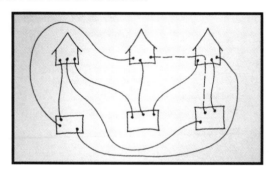

The challenge is to connect each house to each of the three utilities using ropes as the connection lines. Local laws however prohibit utility lines passing over each other, so for the sake of this puzzle, no rope can pass over any other rope. The classic solution shown involves passing one connection line through one of the buildings.

You'll find this and ninety-nine other great puzzles for teams in the book **Teambuilding Puzzles**
ISBN 978-0-7575-7040-7 (www.kendallhunt.com)

3-2 Sliders

I learned many of these puzzles while attending 4-H events in Ohio. Some are more than one hundred years old! Instead of drawing these puzzles on paper and using pennies as markers, consider make a super size version with a long rope, using knots for the various positions along the rope (dots) and paper plates or flying discs (Frisbee™) for the marker.

For the Five Point Star, start at any open position (dot), then count three places and drop your marker. Marked positions may be counted, but not used as a starting position. The goal here is to place nine markers on the star.

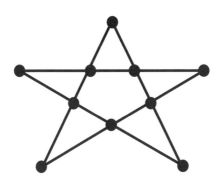

For the clock (with twelve positions), start at any open position, count four in either direction and drop your marker. Marked positions may be counted, but not used as a starting position. The goal is to place nine markers on the clockface.

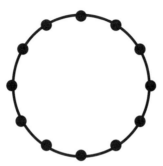

The challenge of the Eight Point Star (possibly the easiest of these puzzles), is to place seven markers on the star. Start at any open position, slide the marker along the length of the line and drop the marker at the end of the line.

3-3 Make a Knot

This classic challenge has been around forever! Pick up a piece of rope and tie an overhand knot in it without letting go of the rope or changing your hand position on the rope.

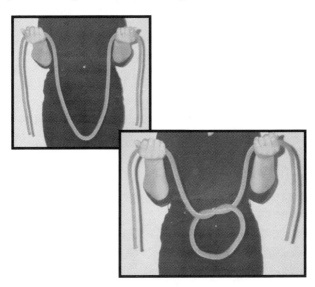

The teachable moment in this rope game is the value of planning ahead. If you cross your arms prior to picking up the rope, when you unfold your arms, the rope will form an overhand knot!

3-4 The 15th Object

You can use any fifteen objects for this challenge, including short pieces of rope. The rope 'worms' in the Rope Games kit work perfectly.

Begin by placing fifteen objects in a line between two players. One player begins the game by removing one, two or three of the objects. The second player then has the choice of removing one, two or three objects. This selection process continues with each partner trying NOT to take the very last object (number fifteen).

The trick of this game is to control (take) the tenth object. You can insure this by also taking the sixth object. And you can insure taking the sixth object by taking the second object. If you control objects two, six and ten, you control the game.

Once players have learned the strategy of winning with fifteen objects, change the game by using fourteen (or sixteen) objects instead. To win at fourteen objects, you'll need to control objects one, five and nine. For sixteen objects, you'll need to control objects three, seven and eleven.

Creating a Teachable Moment

My friend and colleague Kirk Weisler was invited to assist with a wilderness therapy program in a remote area of the Rocky Mountains in January. After a long travel by four wheel drive vehicle, snowmobile, and eventually snowshoes, Kirk and a replacement set of counselors met up with a dozen or so at-risk youth participants of the program. While the outgoing counselors were packing up to leave, Kirk sensed the need to bond the new counselors with the young 'I'm too cool for you' program participants. He gathered fifteen short pieces of rope and placed them on a table in the somewhat cramped main lodge. "I've got a game," he said, "and it takes knowledge and skill. Who wants to play?" One of the young participants accepted Kirk's offer and sat down opposite him at the table. Kirk explained the rules of the challenge and in the first round, Kirk won (no surprise there). At this point, a few of the other participants began to gather around and watch the game.

Round two, Kirk wins again. But this time, there is some conversation amongst the participants. Round three, Kirk wins again. But something is definitely happening. At this point,

Kirk asks the group, "so why do I win, every time?" After a brief discussion and various comments from the group, both respectful and some less than, someone offered, "you know something we don't." Bingo, thought Kirk, now is the time for a teachable moment.

"Who else around here knows things that you don't right now?" Kirk asked. Eventually the counselors were identified. "The good news here," said Kirk, "is that I want you to be able to win at this game. I want you to beat me. I want you to be able to win, every time. All you need is some knowledge. Knowledge is power, and I want you to have some. Now these counselors that are here with you, they have some knowledge too, and the really great news is, they want to share it with you. They want you to win in the biggest game of all, life itself."

At this point, Kirk explained that there were 'key' objects in this game, and that those who controlled those 'keys' controlled the outcome of the game. He also talked about keys to life, and how they controlled the outcome of that 'game.' This simple game opened the door to an outstanding experience for Kirk and the program participants too. Knowledge is power. Get some!

3-5 Pencil Pushers

This activity is one of the most physically challenging in this book. Begin by creating a rope boundary line. Provide each group of three or four players with a single unsharpened pencil.

The challenge is for each group to push their pencil the farthest distance, with only their hands touching the floor beyond the rope line. If any portion of a players body touches the floor past the boundary line, that attempt is disqualified and the group is invited to try again. Teams must be able to place the pencil and return behind the line without touching the floor with anything except their hands.

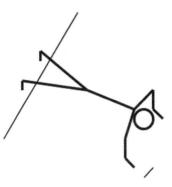

3-6 That's My Hat

You will need a knotted Raccoon Circle for each group of four players for this competitive game of strength and strategy. Begin by inviting players to grasp the Raccoon Circle with one hand, and gently lean outwards away from this square configuration. Next, place one hat about 6 feet (2 meters) away from each player (four hats total at roughly 90 degrees to each other).

The competitive challenge in this activity is to be the first person to retrieve your hat without letting go of the Raccoon Circle.

3-7 Smell the Rope

In my book, Find Something To Do! I managed to collect over a dozen no prop mind games, which I refer to as *I'm in Games*. Here is another one that requires just a single piece of rope.

Begin with one person holding a rope horizontally between their two outstretched hands. Inform the group that you have managed to acquire a very keen sense of smell. So keen in fact, that you can tell the exact location where any member of the group merely touches a rope. Then, as you depart the group, invite a volunteer to come forward and lightly touch the rope with an index finger somewhere between the hands of the person holding the rope. When ready, return to the group and make a serious attempt at smelling the rope, and of course indicating exactly where it has been touched.

The secret in this activity is for the person holding the rope to wiggle their big toe inside their shoe when you get to the right location on the rope. The audience won't be able to see this subtle motion, but you will!

3-8 Erasable Knots

This knot puzzle comes from the field of topology and knot theory. But don't let the mathematics scare you away. It is a fun challenge even without advanced mathematical skills.

Begin by creating two overhand knots that are a mirror image of each other. The challenge in this consensus building activity is to decide together as a group if combining these two knots would erase each of them or simply form a more complicated superknot. After the group has reached consensus, allow them to manipulate these two knots to discover their true nature.

One of the teachable moments for this activity is a discussion of how to make the right decision when you may not have sufficient information or knowledge to do so.

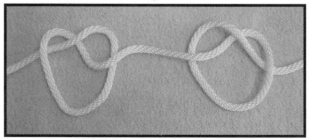

3-9 The Chefalo Knot Trick

From the early 20th century Italian magician (Raffaele Cefalo) comes this unusual knot challenge. If the two ends of this rope are pulled in opposite directions, will the final configuration of the rope contain a knot or no knot?

Amazingly the right side of this unusual knot configuration eliminates the knots in the left side and the final result is a straight line (with no knots at all)! Try it for yourself.

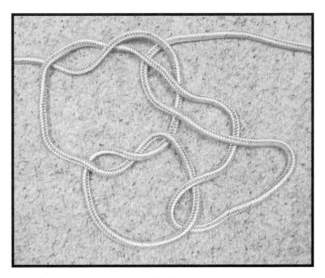

3-10 The BLW Nametag Puzzle

Buckeye Leadership Workshop trains community leaders, teachers, camp counselors and group leaders of all kinds in the fine art of social recreation leadership. The official conference nametage is an Ohio-shaped manipulation puzzle. The challenge is to start with the buckeyes (the official tree of Ohio) on each side of the puzzle (as shown) and manipulate them and the string until you have both buckeyes on the same side.

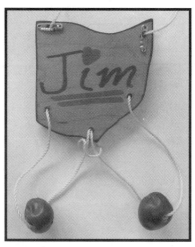

For more information about BLW
visit: www.buckeyeleadership.com

3-11 The Buttonholer

You'll find this puzzling device in many Appalachian toy books. The Buttonholer (also known as a Lapel Needle) is attached to someone's shirt or coat at the start of a party or event, with the removal process left for that person to discover.

The Buttonholer consists of a six inch (150mm) long 1/4" (6mm) diameter dowel rod with a slight point at one end, and a 1/16" (1.5mm) diameter hole drilled through near the other end. A string is now threaded through this hole and knotted into a loop that is too short to pass lover the end of the stick.

To attach, grasp the fabric of someone's shirt, near a collar buttonhole. Pull the fabric through the string loop so that the stick can be threaded through the button hole. To remove the buttonholer, reverse this process.

3-12 Pigs & Pens

Can you place nine pigs into four pens so that each pen contains an odd number of pigs?

Begin by supplying your group with four knotted Raccoon Circles (the pens) and nine pigs (tennis balls are fine, but decorated bleach bottles or plastic piggy banks are a bit more realistic).

All of the following answers are possible solutions to this puzzle.

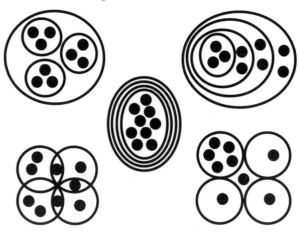

You'll find this and ninety-nine other great puzzles for teams in the book **Teambuilding Puzzles** ISBN 978-0-7575-7040-7 (www.kendallhunt.com)

3-13 Silent Bells

Here is an acoustic activity with magical results. You'll need a metal oven grill and two pieces of string. Tie each piece of string to the metal grillwork. Next wrap each string around one of your index fingers and then put your fingers in your ears (no kidding, really!). Then have a friend strum the grill or tap it gently with a spoon or bump it against another object. The vibration of the grill produces a sound that travels through the strings to your ears. No one else can hear the music except the person holding the strings!

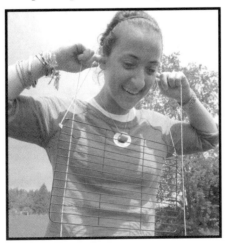

3-14 Line Drawings

See if your next group can create the following line drawings using a single length of rope. For a higher level of challenge, create these designs without allowing the rope to cross itself.

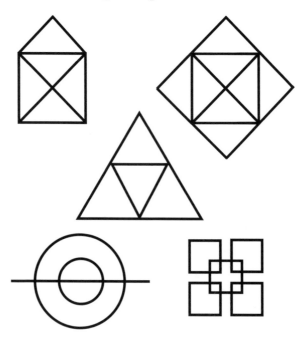

One of the above designs is impossible! Which one?

3-15 Five Rooms

Here is another classic pencil and paper puzzle that can be transformed into a group puzzle. Begin by creating the five room floorplan with sidewalk chalk or duct tape. Then challenge your group to see if they can make a single rope cross each of the wall segments exactly one time.

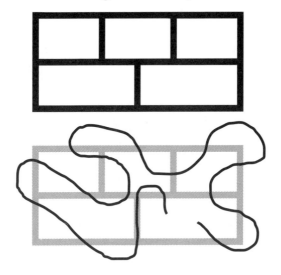

For the solution shown, one of the wall segments is 'crossed' in a different manner than the others. Can you think of other possible solutions?

3-16 Jump Rope Challenge

Here is a group challenge that is easy to explain, but difficult to accomplish! Begin with a collection of ten ropes, varying in length from 1 foot (30 cm) to 10 feet (3 meters), in 1 foot (30 cm) increments. The challenge is for a group to demonstrate their ability to use ALL of the ropes present to jump rope three consecutive times.

For example, a single person could grasp the longest rope by themselves and jump three times in a row or two people could twirl the longest rope while a third person jumps three times between them. The longer ropes in this collection are fairly simple to use. The real challenge will be the shorter pieces.

It is possible for two people to slowly twirl the shortest rope and for a third person to jump over it three consecutive times. I would venture to say that it is almost impossible for any single person to succeed at three consecutive jumps by themself with the shortest rope. A fitting metaphor for teamwork. That which is impossible by ourselves becomes easy when we work together as a team!

Chapter Four
Games Just for Fun

This chapter contains a dozen outstanding rope games. Some are physically challenging, some require skill and dexterity, and some are just plain fun. Enjoy!

No.	Name	Category	Group Size
4-1	Rope Jousting & Last Man Standing	Physical Challenge	Partners and Foursomes
4-2	Horseshoe Golf	Game of Skill	Small
4-3	Ring the Bull	Skill	Individuals
4-4	Tora Tora	Table Fun	Small
4-5	Human Knot	Challenge	Small/Med
4-6	Bump	Challenge	Small
4-7	Steal the Bacon	Game of Skill	Small or Medium

Individuals (1 person)   Small Groups (5-8)
Partners (2 people)   Medium Groups (9-25)
Triads (3 people)   Large Groups (>25)
Foursome (4 people)   XL Groups (>100)

No.	Name	Category	Group Size
4-8	I am the Rope King!	Fun	Medium
4-9	Throwing Knots	Game of Skill	Individuals or Small
4-10	Pirate's Treasure	Challenge Fun	Small Teams
4-11	Texas Roundup	Aerobic Fun	Small or Medium
4-12	Ball Drop	Game of Skill	Individuals

4-1 Rope Jousting

Here is a fun activity for two that requires balance, skill and anticipation of the other player's moves. You will need one unknotted Raccoon Circle for each group of two players.

Begin with both players standing with their own feet side-by-side and about 6 feet (2 meters) apart, grasping opposite ends of the Raccoon Circle (with plenty of slack in between). The object is to make the other person let go of the Raccoon Circle or take a step in any direction.

Last Man Standing

Last Man Standing is a multi-person version of Rope Jousting. For this variation, tie a long rope into a circle by knotting the ends together. Next, invite multiple players to grasp the rope and stand with their own feet side-by-side. On the count of 'go,' players are allowed to tug, pull, relax and otherwise move the rope about. Anyone losing their balance (requiring them to take a step in any direction) or letting go of the rope is out. The last person still holding the rope without having moved their feet is the champion.

4-2 Horseshoe Golf

Horseshoe Golf is a fun, competitive game played at picnics, tailgating parties and summer camps. Each PVC rack is made with 1/2" thickwalled PVC tubes that are either 12 inches (30cm) or 24 inches (61cm) long. You will also need some PVC elbows, T connectors and end caps.

To create the six golf ball bolos, you'll need 21 inches (53cm) of 3/16 inch (5mm) diameter nylon cord. Drill holes through twelve range golf balls (these have solid foam cores), knot the cord on the other side and pull the knot into a countersunk hole. Add a bit of glue to secure the knot in place.

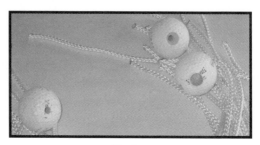

Rules

Space the two PVC racks 15-30 feet apart. The challenge is to toss the golf ball bolos so that they wrap around one of the horizontal PVC bars. Three points for the top bar, two points for the middle and one point for the lower bar. First team to 21 wins. If both teams have a bolo on the same bar, they cancel each other. Bolos knocked off during play do not score any points.

You can find instructions for building and playing Horseshoe Golf at: www.teamworkandteamplay.com

4-3 Ring the Bull

While probably originating as a pub game, this activity belongs everywhere! It is a welcome game of calm and patience in a world of loud noises and high energy.

Ring the Bull requires only two essential components: A metal ring tied to a long piece of string and fastened overhead (to form a pendulum) and a hook protruding from a nearby wall at exactly the right height to catch the ring. Additional wood backing, such as the figure of a bull's head (or the moose head shown here) will help protect your wall from the ring dents likely to be produced by the more enthusiastic players.

The simple task here is to gently release the ring from just the right angle to cause it to swing over and capture the hook.

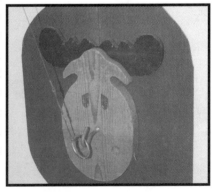

4-4 Tora Tora

This game is one of the oldest in this book and is still fun today. You'll need a plastic condiment bowl, one six-sided die, six strings ten inches (25 cm) long with a wooden bead fastened to one end and a score card.

One person in each group picks up the bowl and rolls the die inside, dropping the bowl and die on top of the six wooden beads. The remaining six members of the group each hold the end of one of the strings. When the roller lifts the bowl, if the die shows a one or six, each of the players pulls their string, while the roller tried to capture as many beads as possible by lowering the bowl quickly. If the die shows a number besides one or six no one should move. After two rolls, the roller and the next person in line switch roles.

Tora Tora is a game of accumulating mistakes. If you pull your string or drop the bowl for any number other than one or six, you receive a letter for each mistake. Make eight mistakes, you spell out Tora Tora and the game is over!

4-5 Human Knot

Here is an exercise in knot removal that doesn't require any rope. Instruct the members of your small group to stand in a circle. Next, invite each person to reach across the circle and grasp right hands with another person and then grasp left hands with a different person. This configuration results in what can be described as a gordian knot. The problem solving opportunity is for this group to un-knot themselves so they are again standing in a circle. The challenge is to do so without anyone in the group letting go.

Depending upon the intensity of the knot formed, some groups may finish quickly while other groups need more time. For especially difficult knots, a visit from the 'Knot Doctor' is possible. The Knot Doctor allows one set of hands to be temporarily disconnected and then immediately re-connected in a different location to facilitate a successful completion to this challenge.

4-6 Bump

Here is one of the more playful Raccoon Circle activities I know. Begin with a small group standing inside a Raccoon Circle. Invite everyone to face the outside of the circle and place their hands on their knees. *"The name of this game is Bump. Last person in the circle, wins! Go!"*

4-7 Steal the Bacon

You can play this game with a variety of soft objects including a bandana or a coiled hank of rope. One person (the protector) stands in the center of the group and guards the object of choice. The remaining members of the group attempt to steal the object without being tagged.

While you can play this game as a traditional playground activity, it also has the potential for teamwork, communication and problem solving. Working together as a team, it is possible to distract the protector long enough for a member of the team to Steal the Bacon.

4-8 I am the Rope King!

The first time I played this game I laughed so hard I couldn't stop.

A large rope circle is formed, with most players standing outside the perimeter. One person volunteers to be the tagger and stands anywhere inside the circle. At the center of the circle is a coiled hank of rope.

The goal of the tagger is to tag anyone moving inside the circle and trade places with them. But during this process two other possibilities can happen. First, two players on opposite sides of the circle can secretly attempt to exchange places. This can temporarily distract the tagger, which makes the next heroic move even more possible. And that is for a single person to run to the center, lift the rope high above their head and yell, "I am the Rope King!" and make it back to their original location (or a new position that opens up) without being tagged.

If they manage to return without being tagged, they are indeed The Rope King!

4-9 Throwing Knots

There is a unique method for creating knots known as Throwing Knots. This solo activity can fill the time spent waiting for a bus, or waiting for the rest of the hikers to catch up, or waiting for a program to begin.

The challenge here is to learn how to throw a knot into an unknotted piece of rope. Let's start with a simple overhand knot. Begin by holding a piece of rope in both hands. Move both hands together, create a twist in the rope, and throw one end of the rope through this twisted loop to form an overhand knot.

For a slightly harder knot, try the Figure Eight. Hold a rope in both hands so that it droops in the middle and forms the letter U. Next, create a twist in the U by twirling it and throwing one end of the rope through the opening in the lower portion of the twirled U. This knot requires one more twisted loop than the overhand knot. With a bit of practice, you should be able to throw a successful knot every time.

A final and very challenging technique for Throwing Knots is to hold one end of a rope and create an overhand knot simply by flipping the bottom end of the rope upward. This one will keep you busy for minutes if not hours. It can be helpful to tie the very end of the rope into a knot, to provide sufficient weight to flip the tail of the rope in place.

4-10 Pirate's Treasure

The first time I saw this activity I laughed so hard I nearly fell over. What a riot! This game requires four people per team. All four are needed to help find a small piece of rope that has been placed in the playing area.

One Seeker - Who is searching for the rope with their eyes closed while listening to the Communicator for directions.

Two Directors - Who each watch the Seeker, but cannot speak. They use hand signals to direct the Communicator.

One Communicator - Who can see and talk, but whose back is to the Seeker. They watch the Directors and shout instructions to the Seeker.

The goal is for the Communicator to help the Seeker find the rope with help from the Directors. This communication activity takes a hilarious turn when a second team of four is introduced. Their blind Seeker however is armed with a long foam pool noodle and has the title of 'Whacker.' For this team, the two Directors instruct the Communicator to tell the Whacker where to find the Seeker and tag him with the foam pool noodle.

4-11 Texas Roundup!

Having replaced the traditional rubber chicken for this activity with a hank of rope, it seems appropriate to change the name from Texas Leghorn to Texas Roundup!

Begin with two groups of about eight players. One team begins by inviting one of their members to throw a coiled hank of rope as far as they can. This first group then forms a small circle, with the thrower running laps around them. The smaller and tighter the circle, the more laps the thrower can accomplish. During this time, all the members of the second team run to retrieve the hank of rope. They line up, and the person retrieving the rope begins passing it down the line with one person passing it over their head and the next person between their legs, alternating like this until the hank of rope reaches the end of the line, at which point the last person yells, *"done!"* and throws the rope as far as they can. The first team counts up the laps they accomplished and runs to retrieve the hank of rope (and the team rolls are reversed). The first team to reach a pre-determined lap count (such as 20 laps), wins!

4-12 Ball Drop

Here is an individual challenge with the feel of a carnival game. You'll need two eyescrews, two pieces of string eight feet (2.4 meters) long, a ping pong ball and a small plastic cup. The challenge here is to use the two strings to maneuver the ping pong ball the length of the strings and then drop the ball into the cup. You can make this activity even more challenging if you ask participants to close one eye (limiting their depth perception).

The television show Minute To Win It has animated game blueprints posted on their website:

www.nbc.com/minute-to-win-it/how-to/

You can also download an extensive Minute To Win It activity guide at multiple websites, including: www. studentministry.org/ym-resources/M2WI_Game_ Activity_Guide.pdf

Chapter Five
Reviewing Techniques
& Closing Activities

"Do we learn from experience? No!
We learn when we reflect on that experience!"
Bert Horwood

Many of the activities presented in this book create valuable *teachable moments*. These are unique opportunities for participants to identify useful skills and practical experiences that they can apply to other situations in their lives. This chapter contains activities and techniques for groups and individuals to discuss, debrief, review and reflect on their progress, especially after a particularly teachable moment. This chapter also contains several closing activities, appropriate for concluding a program, workshop or conference.

Individuals (1 person)   Small Groups (5-8)
Partners (2 people)   Medium Groups (9-25)
Triads (3 people)   Large Groups (>25)
Foursome (4 people)   XL Groups (>100)

Reviewing Techniques
& Closing Activities

No.	Name	Category	Group Size
5-1	Learning Rope	Review	Any
5-2	Worms	Review	Medium
5-3	Step Into the Circle	Review	Medium or Large
5-4	One Word Whip	Fast Review	Any
5-5	Shuffle Left Shuffle Right	Review w/ Movement	Medium
5-6	Fish Bowl	Review	Medium
5-7	The Meter	Review	Small/Med
5-8	Where Do You Stand?	Review Discussion	Any
5-9	Pictograms	Artistic Review	Any
5-10	Why Knots	Discussion	Any
5-11	Virtual Slideshow	Review	Any
5-12	Goal Lines	Review	Medium
5-13	Pass the Knot	Review	Small/Med
5-14	RC Pieces	Closing	Any
5-15	The Final Transmission	Closing	Medium or Large

5-1 The Learning Rope

Here is a brilliant way to help your next group remember all the teachable moments experienced during a training program. You will need a rope about 10 feet (3 meters) long.

Throughout the program, each time a teachable moment is encountered, a member of the group places a single knot onto the learning rope. Before a new knot is added, the group reviews all previous knots to insure that the learning is not lost. At the end of the day, untie each knot as the group identifies and reflects on each teachable moment, or cut the rope between each knot and send the members of your group home with a reminder of the teachable moments they experienced.

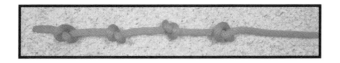

Thanks to Chris Cavert for sharing this innovative technique for remembering the teachable moments encountered during a program. One of the most valuable things I ever learned to do with a rope!

175

5-2 Worms

Here is a reviewing technique that allows the individual opinion of every member of the group to be polled, without requiring anyone to talk. Begin with ten large index cards and add a wide range of words, pictures or other powerful images. Weather patterns, traffic signs, facial expressions (emoticons), character building words, cartoons and scenic photos are all suitable content.

Next, create the 'worms' by cutting short pieces of rope or webbing (4 inches long). At the completion of an activity or program, give each participant in the group one 'worm' and ask everyone to drop their worm at the same time onto one of the picture cards that best represents their experience during the activity. Then begin the debriefing by discussing the pictures with the most worms, the next highest one, or even the ones with no worms.

Worms can also be used during the planning stage of an activity, as a method of voting on various plans, techniques or options. Prepare a few cards that have words like YES & NO, Agree & Disagree, Plan A & Plan B, and Continue Planning or Start Working.

Thanks to Dave Knobbe for sharing this technique.

5-3 Step Into the Circle

I am not a tall person nor do I have a loud voice, so I just step forward to let folks know I have something to share.
Chuck W., Adventure Program Participant

Here is a technique for identifying which members of the group have something to share. Begin by inviting the group to stand around the perimeter of a knotted Raccoon Circle. Next, present the group with a question that you would like for them to consider during their reflection and ask anyone that has a comment to step into the circle.

For a well chosen question, it is likely that several participants will step forward. After each person has had their say, they return to the outside of the circle. The reviewing process continues until no members of the group are left in the circle.

Some members may Step Into the Circle at the very start of the conversation. Others may wait to enter the circle until they have had time to carefully prepare their comments, or to respond to the comments made by another participant.

5-4 One Word Whip

For those situations when you have limited time to debrief, this technique minimizes the conversational aspects of the reviewing process by refining each participant's contribution to a single word.

Begin by inviting group members to stand around the perimeter of a large rope circle, reflect on their recent experiences and find a single word that conveys their experience to the group. Allow the group at least one minute to consider this request. Suggest that each participant initially close their eyes and when they have selected their single word, open their eyes again. This gives the facilitator a visual cue when the group is ready to proceed.

When ready, invite each person to share their One Word with the group.

Once, within a group of 75 international MBA students, a total of 27 different languages and dialects were identified. Each participant was asked to express their experience for the day with one word. Out of curosity, after the first round, participants were asked to repeat the same message in their native languages, many of which required multiple words to convey the same meaning. An interesting lesson in international studies.

5-5 Shuffle Left / Shuffle Right

At the completion of an activity, invite your group
to stand around the perimeter of a rope circle and
teach them this kinesthetic reviewing technique.

Begin by asking participants to shuffle
(step sideways) to the left (clockwise) around the
circle. This motion continues until someone in
the group says, 'stop,' and presents to the group
their thoughts about the recent activity, or a more
specific question framed by the facilitator. When
finished, this person says, "shuffle left,' or 'shuffle
right,' and participants move in that direction until
another person says stop. If at any time the group
makes an entire 360 degree rotation of the circle
without anyone saying stop, it will be time to move
on to the next question or the next activity.

This activity will keep your group in motion and provide
the opportunity for even the quietest voice to be heard.

5-6 The Fish Bowl

Here is a reviewing technique where participants can choose the role they wish to play. There are 'participant' roles and 'observer' roles. First place a rope circle on the ground. Invite 'participants' to have a seat within the perimeter of the circle and 'observers' to stand or sit around the outside perimeter of the circle.

Next pose a question to the group, and invite them to discuss it. It can be hard for observers to remain quiet, especially if a subject is discussed for which they have strong feelings, but the rules remain. It is important to encourage the observers to do just that – observe. At the completion of the discussion by the 'participants,' observers are allowed to voice their observations and comments. If you like, you can ask participants and observers to reverse roles, and allow the other half of the team the opportunity to discuss the same (or a different) topic.

As a facilitator, you can inform your group that their choice is static (once chosen, they must remain in that role throughout the activity), or dynamic (they can move from participant to observer and back again as they wish, simply by moving position). Try both ways and decide for your own facilitation style which method works best for you.

5-7 The Meter

Here is a visual debriefing technique that allows participants to indicate their response to a given question, simply by standing in the position of their choice.

Begin by forming the circular arc of an electronic meter with an unknotted Raccoon Circle. Next, pose a question to the group and indicate the range of possible answers along  the path of the meter. Use your arm to swing from far left to the middle to the far right, indicating these positions as 'no,' 'maybe' and 'yes.' Invite the members of your audience to stand in the position of their choice along this path.

As a facilitator, you can use the meter to obtain a quick measurement of the group, without the need for conversation. What is your personal level of energy right now? *I need a break*, is over here on the left. *I am ready to go*, is over here on the right. Now choose.

5-8 Where Do You Stand?

As a reviewing activity Where Do You Stand is a great way to break a large group (where only a few voices will be heard in the time available) into several smaller groups (with more opportunity for participants to speak and be heard).

Begin by placing several knotted Raccoon Circles nearby. Next, pose a question or reviewing task to the group. Identify which Raccoon Circle represents each typical answer and invite your audience to relocate to the circle of their choice and discuss the answer with others that have gathered there. Invite each group to share their most significant response or thoughts.

5-9 Pictograms

Here is an artistic technique for reviewing. You can use sidewalk chalk, multiple segments of ropes in the Rope Games Kit or even masking tape for this activity. The goal is to create a single picture, image, hieroglyphic or petroglyphic illustration of the team's experience for the day. In this case, a picture is truly worth a thousand words. How would future generations translate your pictogram? How does it capture the essence of today's work?

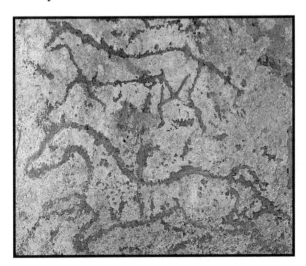

5-10 Why Knots?

Why Knots are short segments of tubular climbing webbing that have been tied into an overhand knot, and then captioned with the word WHY. Create enough of these for every member of your next group. At the completion of the day, invite everyone to take one and reflect on what questions they still have. After a day-long teambuilding event, some folks may wonder:

Why can't more of our training days be like this one?
Why can't we work this well together all the time?
Why do we appreciate days like this one so much?
Why not treat everyone here like family?
Why not appreciate each other more?

You can create your own Why Knots with 10 inch (25cm) long segments of tubular webbing. Choose a light color for the webbing and a dark color permanent marker to write the word WHY.

Thanks to Chris Cavert for sharing yet another great reflection technique.

5-11 The Virtual Slideshow

Here is a visual technique for reviewing that requires no equipment at all. With the group comfortably seated, invite participants to imagine that they had a digital camera throughout the program and were encouraged to take phtographs of their favorite moments of the day. Using the virtual slideshow imaginary 'clicker' they can fast-forward to show their favorite photograph. "If you look at this slide, you'll see our group working out the Disconnected puzzle." CLICK!

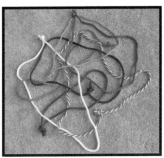

The Virtual Slideshow is an excellent way to encourage participants to share more information during a debriefing or reviewing session. Once they have a picture in mind, it is an easy task to talk about the content of the photo at length.

5-12 Goal Lines

In the first chapter of this book, the activity Goal Lines was used to help individuals set personal goals for their day. At the completion of the day, repeating this activity allows each person individually and the team collectively to assess whether or not they achieved their goals.

Often participants remark that although they may not have reached a specific goal for the day, they did in fact achieve other worthy results and so may wish to modify their original goals. Or, they may wish to tie additional knots in their rope to reflect some of the other learnings they experienced.

If practical, allow your participants to take their Goal Lines home with them, as a reminder of the day, the goals they achieved, and perhaps most importantly, a reminder of those goals that still require additional work to accomplish.

If you happen to use the 'spokes' formation of group goal lines, ask your group to walk the length of their individual ropes together, which will place them all in the center of the circle. A fitting location for the conclusion of the program.

5-13 Pass the Knot

Provide a single knotted Raccoon Circle for each group of five to eight participants. Invite the group to slowly pass the knot to the right around the circle. The knot in this case is rather like a 'talking stick.' That is, whoever has the knot in their possession can say, 'stop,' and share their comments with the group. After speaking, the knot is again passed to the right and continues until another person stops the knot in order to address the group. Continue until all that would like to speak have been given the chance.

Be sure to allow the knot two complete revolutions of the circle at the very end of this activity. Some folks require some silent time to think and compose their thoughts.

5-14 Raccoon Circle Pieces

At the very first Raccoon Circle workshop I attended with Dr. Tom Smith, Tom did a very interesting thing, something I had never seen before, and for me, it was a very powerful experience. At the conclusion of the workshop, Tom presented the single Raccoon Circle we had used for dozens of activities. Everyone in the group had touched this circle at one time or another. Everyone had been supported by it, educated by it, and connected through it to everyone else in the group.

Tom took a bunch of permanent markers and invited each of us to write our names or perhaps contribute a single word to the Raccoon Circle. Next, he produced a hunting knife and began the task of cutting the Raccoon Circle into a dozen or so smaller pieces, and then presented each person in the group with one of these segments. A momento of our time together. A reminder of what we had learned, discovered, achieved and experienced together. A pleasant reminder of a day well spent in the company of others. To this day, I still have that piece!

5-15 The Final Transmission

This final activity is one of my all-time favorites. A musical ceremony that allows nearly every member of the group to connect with each other.

Distribute several knotted Raccoon Circles and invite groups of eight people to grasp each one. Next invite each group to close their eyes and lean back slightly, balancing the circle. Now play your favorite inspirational song. During the song, invite your audience to open their eyes and visually connect with everyone in their circle. Then, ask everyone to hold on with only their left hand and walk (pinwheel) to the right. This movement will look like large gears spinning near each other. From this position, invite participants to raise their hands and high five the members of other circles as they pass. Reverse directions occasionally. Finish the song with the members of each circle looking inward.

Some of my favorite songs for this activity include: The Theme from The Lion King (The Circle of Life), Circles by Harry Chapin, Circle of Friends by Paul Winter, and Will the Circle Be Unbroken? (traditional artists).

For even more processing, debriefing, reviewing and reflection activities, see the following resources:

A Teachable Moment - A Facilitator's Guide to Processing, Debriefing, Reviewing and Reflection by Jim Cain, Michelle Cummings & Jennifer Stanchfield, Kendall/Hunt Publishers (www.kendallhunt.com) 1-800-228-0810.

The Active Reviewing Website Roger Greenaway's outstanding website with an incredible amount of information related to reviewing, including a paper entitled *Reviewing With Ropes*. (www.reviewing.co.uk)

Processing the Experience: Strategies to Enhance & Generalize Learning, John Luckner and Reldan Nadler, Kendall/Hunt Publishers.

Reflective Learning: Theory and Practice by Sugarman, Doherty, Garvey and Gass, Kendall/Hunt Publishers.

The Art of Experiential Group Facilitation - Tips and Tools, Jennifer Stanchfield, WoodnBarnes Publishing.

Chapter Six
Bonus Activities

While most of the activities presented in this book fit into neat categories like icebreakers, teambuilding activities, puzzles, games and reviewing techniques, several span more than one of these categories and may also require additional equipment beyond a few simple pieces of rope. I hope you will enjoy these unique rope activities that go beyond the traditional boundaries of rope games.

Bonus Activities

No.	Name	Category	Group Size
6-1	Rope Gymnastics	Physical Challenge	Individuals
6-2	Slacklines	Balance	Individuals
6-3	Tangloids	Puzzle	Partners
6-4	Rope Burn	Challenge	Small
6-5	Team Bowdrill	Teamwork	Small/Med
6-6	Pendulum Motion	Science & Technology	Small/Med
6-7	Hiking Ropes	Trail Fun	Individuals
6-8	Story Ropes	Discussion	Any
6-9	Frozen Knots	Challenge	Any
6-10	More Rope Games	Challenges Initiatives	Small or Medium

Individuals (1 person)	Small Groups (5-8)
Partners (2 people)	Medium Groups (9-25)
Triads (3 people)	Large Groups (>25)
Foursome (4 people)	XL Groups (>100)

6-1 Rope Gymnastics

Inuit Rope Gymnastics (Qajaasaarneq) is a series of movements on two horizontal ropes, which mimic the movements required by an open water kayaker. There are a total of seventy-four different moves which demand and develop balance, strength, agility, flexibility, coordination and pain tolerance.

For more information about this activity, see:

Video clips at the Qajaq USA website:
  www.qajaqusa.org/movies/movies.html

The physical aparatus for this activity is described in the article *Maligiaq Makes Waves on his US Visit*, by John Heath, Sea Kayaker Magazine, June 2000.

A DVD showing these techniques can be purchased from Tom Sharp c/o Dubside 16410 84th Street NE #427 Lake Stevens, WA 98258 tom@dubside.net

There are NO ropes in the Rope Games kit
that are appropriate for this activity!

6-2 Slacklines

This modern activity demands and develops balance and coordination. In Slacklining, a horizontal rope or cargo strap is stretched between two trees or anchor points. The setup tension is largely a matter of personal preference. Beginners often prefer higher tension initially.

The challenge is for a person to walk the length of the Slackline while carefully balancing themselves. Spotters are essential for beginners, and a good idea at all times. If you feel yourself becoming unbalanced, it is best just to step down from the Slackline rather than struggling to stay on. You can immediately step back on again and continue on your journey to the far end of the Slackline.

One of the best features of Slacklining is that each attempt takes only a few seconds and new Slackliners begin to see improvements in balance and distance traveled quickly.

For more information on Slacklining, search the word Slackline on your web browser. There are many commercial Slackline kits available, and several websites which show you how to create your own.

There are NO ropes in the Rope Games kit
that are appropriate for this activity!

6-3 Tangloids

'Problems worthy of attack, prove
their worth by fighting back!'
                                Piet Hein

Here is a fascinating manipulation puzzle for
the kinesthetic/logical learner in your group.
Piet Hein invented this activity as a way of
demonstrating the mathematics of braiding.

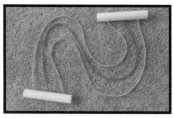

Begin by connecting three different
color cords and two PVC tubes together as
shown. Partners each grasp one PVC tube. The
game begins when one partner makes any three
'moves' with their tube. They can invert, twist,
rotate and otherwise tangle the three ropes as they
wish. The challenge for the second partner is to
'undo' the moves of the first partner, in three or
less moves, and return the ropes to their original
configuration.

6-4 Rope Burn

Camp Olympia in Trinity, Texas has some very creative programming ideas. At the start of each staff training week, two teams compete in an activity they call Rope Burn. In the middle of a sand volleyball pit (a safe place for a campfire), two teams race to collect nearby materials for a campfire. The first team to build a fire and have that fire burn through a rope tied between two metal fence posts wins!

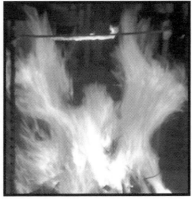

The two activities presented here include an element of fire and require appropriate safety measures. Be sure to have a fire extinguisher nearby.

6-5 Team Bowdrill

While there are many
techniques for starting
a fire without a match,
the bowdrill technique
is both effective and
unique. This technique
can typically be
performed by a single
person.

   Could a Team Bowdrill be a faster or
more effective way to start a fire, or to build a
team? See for yourself!

6-6 Pendulum Motion

I happen to have had more than my share of math courses. I guess that is just part of being an engineer. Recently however, Science, Technology, Engineering and Math (STEM) has been getting more notice in schools and youth programs. Here is an activity for exploring the relationship between math and physics.

Give each group of five students the following props: 6 feet of string, a thumbtack, several metal washers, a yardstick or measuring tape, a protractor, some masking tape and a stopwatch.

Next, challenge them to experimentally design a pendulum that has a period (T) of exactly two seconds. The mathematical equation that defines this length (in inches) is:

$$\text{Length} = T^2 * g \, / \, (2*Pi)^2$$

T=2 second, g=386.088 in/sec^2 and Pi = 3.1416

Interestingly, the weight of the washers have no effect on the period of oscillation for small angles (less than 30 degrees). The length calculated from the above equation is 39.119 inches. This is the distance from the thumbtack anchor point to the center of the metal washers (the center of gravity). What length would produce a 1 second period? Half this length? No, the correct answer is 9.78 inches.

6-7 Hiking Ropes

Jerry Elliott spent a lifetime teaching and sharing ideas for creative recreation programming. Jerry was a friend of mine for many years and he once told me that anytime he traveled with groups on extended hikes and camping trips, he always gave each participant a length of rope at the very start of the expedition. Participants would use these ropes to practice their knot tying skills and for various camp related needs such as pitching a tent, tying up their food bags, tying their canoe to the dock and for several of the games in this book, including Rope Jousting, Steal the Bacon and Throwing Knots, which can be found in Chapter 4.

6-8 Story Ropes

While searching for even more things to do with rope, I found a website dedicated to using a variety of simple things to create a story rope. Visit this website for yourself and see if you don't think this is a truly powerful idea - one that can change the world! You can also find a video here, photographs and dozens of stories of the Story Ropes experience.

www.margemalwitz.blogspot.com

For even more creative ideas for storytelling, see *Show Me A Story - Craft Projects and Activities to Spark Storytelling* by Emily Neuburger, ISBN 978-1-6034-2987-7.

6-9 Frozen Knots

For a summer camp wacky olympics competition we once froze T shirts in blocks of ice, and then challenged groups to thaw these as quickly as possible. The winners were the first team to have one of their group members wear the T shirt.

Karl Rohnke once shared with me that, *"anything worth doing is worth over-doing!"* With that spirit in mind, here is my updated ice block challenge. Take several identical pieces of rope, about 40 inches (1 meter) in length, and tie an identical variety of knots in each piece. Next immerse each rope in a separate container of water and freeze these containers overnight.

You now have several frozen knots. The challenge for each team is to quickly remove the rope from the frozen block of ice and untie the knots. The first team to present their rope with all knots removed is the winner.

Who knows? You might see the Frozen Knot challenge at a future Association for Challenge Course Technolgoy (ACCT) Builder Olympics competition.

6-10 More Ideas for Rope Games

While writing this book, I discovered many interesting rope activities. But I am always looking for more. Perhaps you too will be eager to find other rope games. To help you with your quest, here is a brief list of several unique rope activities and where to find them.

Flash Flood and *Blind Man's Cure* can be found in the book *Into The Classroom* by Mitchell Sakofs and George Armstrong. Both of these teambuilding challenges require strong climbing ropes.

A Frames are giant wooden A's with long ropes. A team of belayers helps one person navigate (walk) using the A Frame. You'll find a description in the book *Silver Bullets* by Karl Rohnke.

A *Monkey's Fist* is a cord craft that is very unique. Instructions (including video) can be found online.

Chinese Jump Rope uses an elastic band instead of a rope. You can find directions in the *Jump Rope Book* by Elizabeth Loredo, and more information online.

Boardwalkers are long boards with rope handles. You can find building instructions in the book *Teamwork & Teamplay* by Jim Cain and Barry Jolliff.

While typically conducted with a bamboo pole, *The Limbo* can be performed with a rope held between two people. The best music for this activity, Limbo Rock by Chubby Checkers.

A *Bull Roarer* or *Fluttermill* is a shaped piece of wood and a long string that makes a unique sound when twirled overhead. You can find instructions in the *Foxfire Six* book by Eliot Wigginton.

You can find Rope Art at www.Pinterest.com.

Riddle: A horse is securely tied to a 20 foot rope. A mound of alfalfa is 30 feet away. Somehow the horse is able to eat the alfalfa even though the rope does not stretch or break. How is this possible? *Answer:* The other end of the rope isn't tied to anything.

Riddle: If you take three ropes from seven ropes what do you have? *Answer:* You have the three ropes your took. If the question had been how many ropes do you have left, that answer would have been four ropes.

Question: The Devil's Rope is another name for a well-known farm item (that is not actually a rope). Name the item. *Answer:* Barbed Wire.

Chapter Seven
The Top Ten List

Here is the list of my absolute favorite rope activities. This collection never fails to deliver when presented to groups of all kinds. You will find descriptions of each activity in their respective chapters.

Activity	Category	Chapter
Bull Ring	Teamwork	2
Not Knots	Teamwork	2
Over Here!	Icebreaker	1
2B or Knot 2B	Teamwork	2
15th Object	Problem Solving	3
Horseshoe Golf	Games for Fun	4
10x10x10	Teamwork	2
Ring the Bull	Games for Fun	4
The Learning Rope	Reviewing	5
Wrapped Around My Finger	Icebreaker	1

How to Make Your Own Rope Games Equipment

Here are descriptions of how to make many of the props mentioned in this book. You can also purchase a Rope Games Kit (teamworkandteamplay.com or training-wheels.com for more information). You can find instructions for making some of this equipment (such as horseshoe golf, story ropes & raccoon circles) online.

Raccoon Circles are 15 foot (4.5 meter) long segments of 1" (25.4mm) wide tubular climbing webbing. 1/2" (12mm) and 3/4" (19mm) widths are also available. You can buy this material by the foot (meter) at most outdoor stores that sell climbing gear, and also at horse tack shops. One circle accomodates up to 8 adults (10 children).

Bull Rings are 1.5" (38mm) diameter harness (metal) rings that have been welded together. These will easily carry a tennis or golf ball. Attach (knot) up to twelve strings, one for each participant.

3-D Bull Rings are made with six strings and a 1-1/2" diameter PVC tube about 6 inches (152mm) long (instead of a metal ring). Two small holes are drilled into the tube about 1/4" (6mm) apart for each string.

The **Plastic Cones** used for Bull Ring are recycled commercial sewing machine thread spools. Find someone in your community that does high volume sewing and they will know about these spools.

Goin' Fishin' props are made from a wooden alphabet block (pine), with six holes drilled completely through. After passing six strings through these holes, nearby strings are knotted together and then six different metal hardware hooks are attached.

Handcuffs are made from 1/4" (6mm) diameter soft cotton clothesline. Each handcuff is 60 inches (152cm) long. A slip knot loop is tied at each end.

Long Ropes are 3 strand multiline or climbing rope, 3/8" (9mm) diameter by 50 feet (15 meters) long.

Short Ropes are Derby ropes available at many hardware stores, approximately 1/2" (12mm) in diameter by about 8 feet (2.4 meters) long.

The **Worm Hole** is 40 inches (1 meter) of 3/16" (4mm) elastic shock (bungie) cord. It is **ABSOLUTELY ESSENTIAL** to tie a knot that cannot work loose.

The elastic band for **SNAP** is standard sewing elastic, 3/4" (19mm) wide by 40 inches (1 meter) long. Use a water knot (the same as used with Raccoon Circles) to connect the ends together.

Worms are leftover rope, cord or webbing segments that have been cut to 4" (10 cm) lengths. If you happen to use a rope that unravels, you will need to tie a knot at each end to prevent fraying.

String used in this book is standard nylon (kitestring) or cotton (packaging string) or neon colored mason line (available in most hardware stores). You'll need a spool of at least 200 feet (61 meters).

Parachute Cord is used to create the 2B or Knot 2B puzzle. Military stores sell this type of rope. There are several websites that can show you how to make a survival bracelet using parachute cord.

Horseshoe Golf requires 1/2" PVC tubing and connectors for the two stands. The bolos are made from two range golf balls with 5mm cord segments 21 inches (53cm) long. Free detailed directions are available at: www.teamworkandteamplay.com.

The **Lycra Tube** used for Team Yoga is made from 15 feet (4.5 meters) of nylon tricot lycra that has been sewn into a circular tube. More activities using the lycra tube at: www.teamworkandteamplay.com.

In addition to rope you can add index cards, tennis balls, pens, playing cards, dice and duct tape to round out your Rope Games kit.

Chapter Eight
References & Resources

You will find the following information in this final chapter of this book.

Reference Books – A Bibliography

Other Books by Jim Cain

The Rope Games Kit

About Jim Cain and Teamwork & Teamplay

About the Easy-as-1-2-3 Series of Books

The Value of a Little Red Rope

For More Information

Reference Books
A Bibliography

In addition to the 123+ rope activities in this book, here are several additional resources that contain even more ideas for activities with string, rope, shock cord, webbing and other types of cordage.

The Rope Games Kit, a valuable collection of the ropes and props detailed in the book ROPE GAMES by Jim Cain. Visit the T&T website for more information at: www.teamworkandteamplay.com.

The Ropework & Ropeplay Kit, a backpack collection of ten varieties of rope, webbing and other cordage for facilitating over 300 activities. Available from: www.training-wheels.com (1-888-553-0147).

The Revised and Expanded Book of Raccoon Circles, Jim Cain & Tom Smith, ISBN 0-7575-3265-9. Hundreds of activities using only a piece of tubular climbing webbing. You can also download a free collection of Raccoon Circle activities at: www. teamworkandteamplay.com.

Cowboy Roping and Rope Tricks, Chester Byers, Dover Publications, NY. ISBN 0-486-25711-8 "Chet knows more about roping than any man in the world," said Will Rogers.

Fun With String - A collection of games, knot work & magic, Joseph Leeming. A classic collection of interesting things to do with string and rope.

Ranch Rope – A Practical Guide to Traditional Roping, Buck Brannaman, Western Horseman, Colorado Springs, CO USA ISBN 0-911647-54-6

Self-Working Rope Magic - 70 Foolproof Tricks, Karl Fulves, Dover Publications, New York, NY USA ISBN 0-486-26541-2

The Knots Puzzle Book, Heather McLeay, ISBN 1-55953-000-6 Dozens of ideas for turning any piece of rope into a puzzle to be solved!

The Jump Rope Book, Elizabeth Loredo, ISBN 0-7611-0448-8 Dozens of jumping styles, rhymes, stories and ideas for creative rope jumping.

Knots and How to Tie Them, Walter B. Gibson, ISBN 0-517-09369-3 A guide to tying from the simplest knot to the fanciest rope work.

The Practical and Entertaining Art of Tying Knots, Allan & Paulette Macfarlan, ISBN 0-486-24515-2

You can find additional rope activities, and much more, at the Teamwork & Teamplay website:

www.teamworkandteamplay.com

Other Books
Authored By Jim Cain

Teamwork & Teamplay, Jim Cain & Barry Jolliff, 1998, ISBN 978-0-7872-4532-0. Winner of the Karl Rohnke Creativity Award from AEE. 417 pages of adventure-based learning activities. Considered by many as 'the' essential teambuilding text.

The Revised and Expanded Book of Raccoon Circles, Jim Cain & Tom Smith, 2006, ISBN 978-0-7575-3265-8. Hundreds of activities using only a few pieces of tubular webbing.

Teambuilding Puzzles, Jim Cain, Chris Cavert, Mike Anderson & Tom Heck, 2009, ISBN 978-0-7575-7040-7. One hundred puzzles for teams that build valuable life skills.

A Teachable Moment, Jim Cain, Michelle Cummings & Jennifer Stanchfield, 2005, ISBN 978-0-7575-1782-2. A Facilitator's Guide to Activities for Processing, Debriefing, Reviewing and Reflection.

Essential Staff Training Activities, Jim Cain, Clare Marie Hannon & Dave Knobbe, 2009, ISBN 978-0-7575-6167-2. Tips, activities, ideas and suggestions for making your staff training active, engaging, memorable, effective and fun!

It's all in the Cards, Jim Cain (available 2015). Dozens of team and community building activities that you can create with just index and playing cards.

The above six books are available from Kendall/Hunt Publishers of Dubuque, Iowa USA at 1-800-228-0810 or www.kendallhunt.com.

The Big Book of Low-Cost Training Games, Jim Cain & Mary Scannell, 2012, ISBN 978-0-07-177437-6. Powerful activities that explore training topics. Available at www.MHProfessional.com and also as an electronic book from Amazon.com.

Find Something To Do! Jim Cain, 2012, ISBN 978-0-9882046-0-7 Jim's collection of powerful activities with no equipment at all. Easy as 1-2-3!

ROPE GAMES, Jim Cain, 2013, ISBN 978-0-9882046-1-4. A collection of Jim's favorite, newest and best team and community building activities using ropes from around the world. Easy as 1-2-3!

You can purchase single copies of the above two Easy as 1-2-3 Series books at: www.training-wheels.com or by calling 1-888-553-0147. For multiple copies or bulk orders, contact the author directly at:
jimcain@teamworkandteamplay.com

The Rope Games Kit
from Teamwork & Teamplay

Here is a listing of the wonderful things you'll find
in the Rope Games kit from Teamwork & Teamplay.
You can see a photo of this kit on page 8.

One Traditional Bull Ring (metal ring with strings)
One Going Fishin' Tool (hooks, block & strings)
One 3-D Bull Ring (PVC tube with strings)
One Plastic Cone Stand for Bull Ring
One Long Rope (40-50 feet long)
One Short Rope (6-10 feet long)
Twelve Rope Handcuffs
One SNAP Band (elastic band)
One Worm Hole (elastic shock cord)
One Spool of String (200+ feet long)
Three Raccoon Circles (12-15 foot long)
Sixteen Worms (rope or webbing segments)
Two 2B or KNOT 2B Puzzles (parachute cord)
One copy of the book *Rope Games* by Jim Cain
A drawstring stuff sack or totebag to hold everything

For more information about The Rope Games Kit
and other teambuilding books, props and resources,
visit the Teamwork & Teamplay website at:
www.teamworkandteamplay.com

214

About Jim Cain
Teamwork & Teamplay

Dr. Jim Cain is the author of a dozen team and community building texts, including his classic first book, *Teamwork & Teamplay*. He has collected, improvised, researched and created hundreds of activities that build unity, community, connection, leadership and teamwork, and shared them with audiences around the world.

Jim is the creative force behind his company Teamwork & Teamplay and has presented workshops in 47 states and 27 countries (so far). His publications are widely praised, his train-the-trainer programs legendary, his teambuilding props are unique and his group facilitation skills are masterful.

If you would like to invite Jim to make a presentation at your next conference, workshop, training event or program, contact him at:

Jim Cain, Ph.D.
Teamwork & Teamplay
468 Salmon Creek Road
Brockport, New York 14420-9761 USA
Telephone 585-637-0328
Email: jimcain@teamworkandteamplay.com
Website: www.teamworkandteamplay.com

About the

Easy as 1-2-3
Series of Books

Jim Cain and Teamwork & Teamplay are proud to announce the continuation of the 'Easy as 1-2-3' series of books and publications. This innovative series explores a wide variety of team and community building subjects such as painless icebreakers, propless activities, musical activities, teambuilding games with simple props, creative debriefing techniques, leadership activities, games every teacher/trainer/facilitator/groupleader should know, table games, rope games and more!

Each publication contains concise and useful information with just the right amount of photographs and suggestions to help you use these activities successfully at your next program.

One of the next books in the series is entitled Sticks & Stones, Paper & String, Puzzles & Games & Wonderful Things - Fun Stuff to do with Simple Things, and will be available soon.

Watch the Teamwork & Teamplay website for more information about the Easy as 1-2-3 series of books and publications.

www.teamworkandteamplay.com

The Value of a Little Red Rope

One of the greatest joys of being a facilitator is when a teambuilding group experiences the power of a truly significant teachable moment. Over the span of my career, I've been blessed to have experienced several of these peak moments. One of my favorite moments happened a few years ago during a teambuilding program for a small software development company.

I had prepared the consensus building activity Not Knots (which you can find in Chapter Two of this book). Two camps had developed during the activity. On one side, those that believed a knot would occur when the ends of a red rope were pulled and on the other side, those that believed no knot would occur.

Just prior to actually pulling the ropes and revealing the answer, I modified the rules just a bit. I made it acceptable for any member of the group to change sides at any time.

As I slowly pulled the ends of the rope, and the solution revealed itself, the new CEO of this company said, *"somebody give me a cell phone,"* and walked off into the woods for some privacy. I debriefed the activity with the remaining group members, and then called for a short break.

A few minutes later, when the CEO reappeared, it was obvious that he had experienced an epiphany of sorts. When I asked him what was going on, he said:

"I'm the new CEO of this company. Two months ago I made a decision about a June project, but last week I found a better method. This was during the time when some national political candidates were waffling on some critical decisions – and I didn't want my board members to think that I was a waffler, so I stuck with my earlier decision, even though I knew that my earlier decision was the wrong one. This activity

has given me permission to do the right thing, not necessarily the easy thing. I don't care what you do for the rest of the day. For me personally, this one activity has made the whole day worth it!"

It was obvious that this particular CEO was agonizing over his earlier decision, and this one activity helped him cure the source of his pain. And best of all, the board members present supported him in this decision.

At that point I realized that one of the greatest things I could do for a group as a facilitator was to help them explore and perhaps even solve one of the situations that was causing them pain. For the CEO in this story, eight feet of red rope made all the difference.

It is not everyday that such a significant and profound teachable moment occurs within the groups I facilitate. But it did on this day. In many ways, even without knowing it beforehand, I presented an activity that had the potential to cure the 'pain' that the CEO was experiencing related to his earlier decision. I believe that many of the activities in this book have the potential to explore and cure some of the many problems groups face in the world today, including issues of communication, trust, teamwork, creative problem solving, conflict resolution and many, many others. Wisely used, nearly any of the activities in this book can become the catalyst for changing the attitudes, behaviors and perhaps even the culture of the groups you work with, and those you play with as well.

So, what teachable moment will you explore with your next group?

If you enjoyed this story of creating teachable moments with rope, you might also enjoy the story found in Chapter Three on pages 143 and 144. Read and learn how fifteen short pieces of rope created a significant teachable moment for a dozen at-risk youth.

More Rope Games

If you enjoy this collection of Rope Games and you'd like to recommend other games, activities or things to do with rope, string, webbing and various kinds of cordage, I'd love to hear from you. Send me an email and a photograph (if available) of an idea you would like to share and I'll send you some electronic files filled with more games and teambuilding activities in return.

jimcain@teamworkandteamplay.com

A Special Thanks to Markel

Markel is pleased to once again partner with Dr. Jim Cain on his latest book, ROPE GAMES - 123 Activities That Create Powerful Teachable Moments.

This book is full of ideas for keeping children and adults occupied and safe when you need to engage a group with some powerful activities that range from problem solving and teamwork to communication and trust. Markel is proud to sponsor an advocate of risk management solutions.

As a successful innovator in the camp and youth recreation insurance industry, Markel encourages the positive and fun tactics that ROPE GAMES delivers. How might you engage and entertain children with a few pieces of rope while waiting out a thunderstorm, when the bus breaks down, or if a parent is late for pick-up? The activities in this book provide a positive and fun way to manage circumstances safely—something Markel greatly encourages.

We hope this book provides many fun and safe experiences and enhances your leadership toolbox with the ability to do 123 things with a few simple pieces of rope or string.

 To learn more about Markel and other youth-related organizations we insure, please visit: markelinsurance.com

Notes

Thank you for reading
ROPE GAMES

If you would like to obtain additional copies of this book or other books by Jim Cain, or invite Jim to speak at your next conference, workshop, staff training event or program, contact him at:

Jim Cain, Ph.D.

Teamwork & Teamplay

468 Salmon Creek Road
Brockport, New York 14420-9761 USA

Telephone 585-637-0328

Email: jimcain@teamworkandteamplay.com

Website: www.teamworkandteamplay.com